COACH OZ - MASTERING THE MENTAL GAME OF HIGH SCHOOL BASEBALL

PROVEN STRATEGIES FOR COACHES AND PLAYERS TO OVERCOME ADVERSITY AND SUCCEED UNDER PRESSURE

SCOTT OSDER

EDITED BY

W J SHEWELOFF

For my mother, Fran.
Your unwavering support has been a constant
from my first game to the present day,
standing on the sidelines, cheering me on.
Thank you for always being there, believing in me,
and sharing this journey from player to coach.
This book is for you.

ABOUT THE AUTHOR

Scott Osder, an accomplished baseball coach with a career spanning multiple decades, has distinguished himself as a leader in both high school and some collegiate baseball. Known for his ability to transform struggling programs into champions, Osder's commitment to his players and his expertise in the sport has earned him the title of CIF Champion Coach and experience at the NCAA Division 1 and 2 levels. Now, as he prepares to write a book about his journey in the world of baseball, Osder aims to share the lessons, victories, and challenges that shaped him as a coach.

Osder's coaching career began to blossom in high school baseball, where he quickly established himself as a turnaround specialist. He turned around, arguably the worst program in the Los Angeles city section over a 20 year span into one of the top eight teams. Under his leadership, the team reached the playoffs every year he was head varsity coach. This role then launched his coaching career at the D1 level at California State University, Northridge.

His time as the **Head Coach at Tamalpais High School** showcased his ability to lead programs to new heights. Under his leadership, Tamalpais achieved its first CIF Championship since 1929 in 2014, with Osder leading a playoff run where his team outscored opponents 13-2 and allowed no earned runs. He also guided Tam to the North Coast Section Division III championship. His coaching style, focused on discipline and fundamentals, transformed the team into a defensive powerhouse, boasting the league's best ERA, fewest walks allowed, and WHIP. In just one year, he improved the team's ERA from 3.08 to 1.81, reduced walks by half, and saw several of his players go on to compete at the collegiate level.

This success carried over into other roles. At **Temecula Valley High School**, Osder led a remarkable turnaround in 2017, taking the team from a 3-22-1 record to a winning 14-12-1 season. His strategic prowess was evident in his ability to defeat top-ranked teams across divisions and raise his team's MaxPreps rating by over 450 spots. Temecula Valley's offense flourished under his leadership, with runs scored increasing by 128% and batting averages rising by 40 points. His ability to build robust defensive units was just as notable, as the team's ERA dropped from 4.04 to 2.31 in one season.

Osder's collegiate coaching experience further solidified his reputation as a transformative leader. As an **Assistant Coach at San Francisco State University** in 2016, he helped the program achieve its most wins in over a decade. The team's defense and offensive stats improved across the board while he was on staff, and his recruiting efforts helped bring in top talent that would continue to elevate the program.

While at San Francisco State, Osder was certified to recruit at the national D2 level and holds several certifications from the National Federation of High Schools, including First Aid Health and Safety for Coaches, Fundamentals of Coaching, and Concussion Protocol. These certifications speak to his dedication not only to winning but also to the safety and well-being of his players, ensuring they are equipped both physically and mentally to succeed.

Throughout his career, Osder has been more than just a coach; he has been a mentor, guiding his players on and off the field. His community outreach efforts, including organizing Little League Challenger Division Day and Tam Earth School Clean-Up Day, reflect his commitment to fostering a sense of responsibility and community among his athletes.

Born with a passion for sports and a keen sense of leadership, Osder's journey began in earnest at **Cal State University, Northridge**, where he earned a Bachelor of Arts in Business and Marketing in 1988. His education laid a strong foundation for his future coaching endeavors, providing him with the strategic mindset needed to excel in a highly competitive field. He later went on to pursue a **Master of Arts in Education and Psychology** from **Pepperdine University** in 2012, further deepening his understanding of player development and motivation, key elements in his coaching success.

As Scott Osder embarks on writing his book, he aims to provide a behind-the-scenes look at what it takes to build winning programs using mental strategies to complement the intricacies of coaching at different levels, affecting the enduring impact of mentorship in sports. With decades of experience and a legacy of turning underperforming teams into champions, Osder's story promises to inspire future coaches, athletes, and sports enthusiasts alike.

Scott resides in Mill Valley, California and has two children, one living in Hawaii and the other residing in San Diego.

CONTENTS

INTRODUCTION

I remember it like it was yesterday. We were in the top of the final inning of a league championship game, holding onto a one-run lead. Our pitcher was in a tough spot — the first two batters got on base, and I could tell his confidence was shaken. He needed a reminder that to get out of the inning, he had to forget what just happened, take a deep breath, and focus on one pitch at a time.

I went to the mound and told him: "Breathe, focus, and execute the next pitch. Then repeat it. Breathe, focus, execute." And that's precisely what he did. He struck out the next two batters and got the last one to fly out, sealing the win for us.

The key lesson he learned that day was about building mental toughness — staying in the moment and letting go of what he couldn't control. From then on, his approach was simple: focus, breathe, execute.

My name is Scott Osder, and I have been coaching youth, high school, and college baseball for 25 years. I've had the privilege of guiding multiple programs with success winning at every stop including a high school baseball championship. My background in education and psychology, with a master's degree in both fields, has given me a unique perspective on the game. This blend of experience and academic knowledge has made me firmly believe in the power of mental strategies in baseball.

This book shares what I've learned over the years. I want to help you become an authority in gameplay and mental strategies in youth, high school, and college baseball.

Drawing on over two decades of hands-on coaching and mentoring thousands of players, I've embedded a wealth of insights and skills within these pages. You'll learn proven methods and techniques designed to elevate your game, along with strategies for coaches' and players' mental preparedness and emotional resilience —key factors that are essential for achieving success on and off the field.

Mental strategies are often the difference between winning and losing. Studies show that mental toughness can account for up to 90% of an athlete's performance. Mentally tough players can handle pressure, stay focused, and bounce back from setbacks. They perform better under stress and make smarter decisions on the field.

For coaches who may feel they don't have a roster full of naturally gifted athletes, the mental strategies in this book provide an effective way to elevate your team's performance. When trained properly, these techniques can help your players compete at a higher level, regardless of their physical talent. I've seen firsthand how teaching these mental strategies can push teams to play beyond their perceived skill level.

The book's structure is straightforward. We'll start with the foundations of mental toughness. You'll learn how to focus and concentrate better. We'll cover emotional regulation and confidence-building techniques. There's a chapter on how parents can support their young athletes. For high school and college athletes, we'll explore advanced mental strategies. You'll also find tips on effective team communication and inspirational stories from my coaching career.

The vision of this book is to provide you with practical, actionable, and research-backed strategies. These strategies will help you excel in baseball and beyond. The lessons you learn here can be applied to various aspects of life, including personal and professional growth.

So, I invite you to fully engage with this material. Practice the strategies and witness the transformative impact on your performance and life. This journey is not just about becoming a better player or coach. It's about becoming a better person, equipped with the mental tools to succeed in any field.

Let's get started. The game is waiting, and so is your potential.

1

FOUNDATIONS OF MENTAL TOUGHNESS

W hen I first started coaching, I had a player named Mike, who was incredibly talented, but struggled with his mental game. During practices, he was great. He trained, free and easy, but come game time, his performance would falter. He would put too much pressure on himself. One day, after a particularly tough game, I sat down with him and asked him to visualize his best practice moments prior to each game. I asked him to control what he could and breathe before each pitch, and that no matter what happened, good or bad, he wasn't coming out of the game and the world wasn't ending. It was a simple exercise, but the results were astounding. Mike's confidence soared, and he became one of the most reliable players on the team. This experience taught me that mental toughness is not just a buzzword; it's a game changer.

The Mental Game: An Overview

Let's dive into the concept of the mental game in baseball. When we talk about the mental game, we're referring to the psychological aspects that influence your performance on the field. It's the ability to stay focused, confident, and composed under pressure. While physical skills are crucial, the mental game often separates the great players from the merely good ones. Mental toughness is consistently performing at your best, regardless of the circumstances. It's about maintaining clarity of mind, resilience, and a positive attitude, even when things aren't going your way.

Mental toughness is different from physical toughness. Physical toughness is about your body's ability to endure and perform physically demanding tasks. Mental toughness, on the other hand, is about your mind's ability to handle stress, pressure, and adversity. The mental resilience allows you to bounce back from setbacks and keep pushing forward. Historical examples of mentally tough baseball players include legends like Derek Jeter and Mariano Rivera. Jeter's work ethic and consistency were unparalleled, and Rivera's mental toughness and resilience made him one of the greatest closers in the game's history.

Now, let's break down the components of mental toughness. First and foremost is focus and concentration. Being able to block out distractions and maintain focus on the task at hand is crucial. Next is confidence and self-belief. Even when the odds are against you, believing in your abilities can make a significant difference. Emotional regulation is another critical component. It's managing your emotions, whether staying calm under pressure or bouncing back from a mistake. All these elements together form the foundation of mental toughness.

Players often face common mental challenges that can affect their performance. Performance anxiety is a big one. The fear of not performing up to expectations can lead to nervousness and mistakes. Then there's the fear of failure, which can be paralyzing. This fear can prevent you from taking risks or trying new things, limiting your growth as a player. Handling pressure situations is another challenge. Whether it's a crucial game or a tight situation, staying composed and performing your best is vital.

This is where mental training comes into play. Mental training involves exercises and techniques designed to improve your psychological skills. Just like physical training, *mental training requires consistent practice and effort*. The benefits are numerous. Mental exercises can help you stay focused, build confidence, and manage stress. Integrating mental training into your regular practice routines allows you to develop the mental toughness needed to excel in baseball and beyond. Whether it's visualization, mindfulness, or positive self-talk, these techniques can help you perform best when it matters most.

How do you start integrating mental training into your routine? It's simpler than you think. Start with small, manageable exercises like deep breathing or visualization. Gradually, as these techniques become second nature, you can incorporate more complex mental strategies. The key is consistency. As you wouldn't expect to build muscle overnight, developing mental toughness takes time and dedication. But the payoff is worth it. You'll find yourself more focused, more confident, and better able to handle the ups and downs of the game.

In this section, we'll cover everything you need to know about the mental game in baseball. You'll learn to build focus and concentration, boost confidence, and regulate your emotions. We'll also discuss common mental challenges and how to overcome them. By the end of this chapter, you'll have a solid understanding of the game's mental aspects and how to train your mind for peak performance. Whether you're a player looking to improve or a coach wanting to inspire your team, these insights will be invaluable.

Building a Strong Mindset

A strong mindset is the backbone of any successful athlete. The mental framework allows players to persevere, adapt, and thrive, no matter the circumstances. For baseball players, *a strong mindset means approaching every game, practice, and challenge with the belief that they can improve and succeed.* This belief is called a growth mindset, contrasting with a fixed mindset. A growth mindset is the understanding that abilities and intelligence can be developed through dedication and hard work. In contrast, a fixed mindset is the belief that talent and intelligence are static traits that cannot change. Players with a growth mindset are more likely to embrace challenges, learn from criticism, and persist in the face of setbacks, while those with a fixed mindset may shy away from challenges and give up easily.

Cultivating a solid mindset takes effort and intentional practice. One effective technique is setting realistic and achievable goals. Break down larger objectives into smaller, manageable tasks. This makes the process less overwhelming and provides frequent opportunities for success, which builds confidence. Another method is practicing positive self-talk. This involves replacing negative thoughts with positive affirmations. Instead of thinking, "I can't do this," encourage yourself with, "I can improve with practice." Developing a routine for mental conditioning is also crucial. This can include daily mindfulness exercises, visualization, or journaling about your goals and progress. Consistency in these practices can significantly strengthen your mental resilience over time.

Coaches play a vital role in fostering a solid mindset within their teams. Encouragement and positive reinforcement are potent tools. A coach's acknowledgment of a player's effort and improvement boosts their confidence and motivation. Creating a supportive team environment is equally important. This means fostering a culture where players feel safe to take risks and make mistakes without fear of harsh judgment. Encourage open communication and team-building activities that promote trust and camaraderie. *When players know their coach and teammates support them, they're more likely to adopt a growth mindset and push through challenges.*

Consider the example of Max Scherzer, a professional baseball player with a strong mindset. Scherzer faced numerous obstacles early in his career, including injuries and inconsistent performance. However, his unwavering determination and growth mindset propelled him to become a three-time Cy Young Award winner. Scherzer's story illustrates the power of a strong mindset. Despite setbacks, he continuously worked on his skills, embraced challenges, and maintained a positive attitude, ultimately achieving remarkable success.

Another inspiring example is Derek Jeter. Known for his work ethic and consistency, Jeter approached every game believing he could improve. He set high standards for himself and his teammates, leading by example. Jeter's strong mindset was evident in his ability to perform under pressure and bounce back from failures. His career is a testament to the importance of mental strength in achieving long-term success in baseball.

In the next part of this book, we'll delve deeper into specific techniques to build a strong mindset. You'll learn how to set realistic goals, practice positive self-talk, and develop a consistent routine for mental conditioning. We'll also explore how coaches can create a supportive environment that nurtures a growth mindset in their players. By adopting these practices, you'll improve your performance on the field and develop mental resilience that will benefit you in all areas of life. The journey to mental toughness is ongoing, but with dedication and the right strategies, you can cultivate a mindset that drives success and fulfillment.

The Power of Visualization in Baseball

Visualization is a game-changer in baseball and is more powerful than many realize. At its core, visualization is creating vivid and detailed images of yourself performing specific actions. Imagine standing at the plate, feeling the bat in your hands, hearing the crowd roar, and seeing the ball leave the pitcher's hand. The principles of visualization involve engaging all your senses to create a mental rehearsal that is as close to reality as possible. This mental practice sends signals to your brain, forming neural pathways like those made during physical practice. Research has shown that visualization improves performance, reduces anxiety, and enhances overall mental readiness. It's not just about picturing success; it's about mentally experiencing the process of achieving it.

To start with visualization exercises, find a quiet space to focus without distractions. Sit comfortably, close your eyes, and take a few deep breaths to center yourself. Begin by visualizing specific game scenarios. For example, imagine yourself at bat, facing a tough pitcher. Picture every detail—the pitcher's windup, the way the ball spins, and the bat making contact. Incorporate all your senses into the visualization. Feel the bat's grip, hear the crowd, and smell the fresh-cut grass. The more vividly you can imagine the scene, the more influential the visualization will be. Spend a few minutes each day on these mental rehearsals, gradually increasing the complexity of the scenarios.

The benefits of visualization for athletes are immense. First, it improves focus and concentration. By mentally rehearsing game situations, you're training your mind to stay locked in, even under pressure. This mental practice can translate into better focus during actual games. Visualization also enhances confidence and self-belief. Seeing yourself succeed in your mind's eye builds a mental image of success, making it easier to replicate on the field. Additionally, visualization helps with the execution of physical skills. Practicing a swing or a pitch can improve muscle memory and coordination, making your movements more fluid and precise during the game.

Real-life examples of successful visualization abound in professional sports. Take, for instance, Michael Phelps, the legendary swimmer. Phelps used visualization to mentally rehearse every aspect of his races, from start to finish. He would visualize potential challenges, like a goggle malfunction, and see himself overcoming them. This mental preparation played a crucial role in his record-breaking Olympic performances. Players like Alex Rodriguez and Derek Jeter have also credited visualization for their success in baseball. Rodriguez, in particular, would spend hours visualizing his at-bats, which helped him stay focused and confident during games. These athletes' stories highlight the transformative power of visualization.

At times, teams get into a slump and have trouble scoring runs. The day after one of those games, we decided to meet before practice and lie in the outfield, which was completely quiet. With our eyes closed, each player would visualize stepping up to the plate, swinging the bat, and getting a hit. From that point on, we took a few minutes before practice to perform this visualization routine whenever we were struggling. It helped us focus and improve our performance.

Incorporating visualization into your training routine doesn't require much time but pays off significantly. Make it a habit, just like physical practice. Start with simple scenarios and gradually add complexity. Encourage your players to embrace this technique and lead by example. Share stories of successful athletes who use visualization to inspire them. Remember, visualization is not a substitute for physical practice but a powerful complement. You can unlock new performance and mental readiness levels by engaging your mind and body. Visualization is a tool that can transform not only your game but also your approach to challenges, both on and off the field.

Developing Mental Resilience

Mental resilience is the backbone of any successful athlete. It's the ability to bounce back from setbacks and maintain performance under pressure. This means staying composed after striking out or making an error in baseball. It's about not letting one foul play affect the rest of your game. Mental resilience allows players to keep pushing forward, even when the odds are against them. It's essential because baseball, like life, is full of ups and downs. The players who can navigate these fluctuations with grace and determination are the ones who ultimately succeed.

Stress management techniques are crucial to enhancing mental resilience. One effective method is deep breathing exercises. When you are in a high-pressure situation, take a few deep breaths to calm your nerves. This simple act can help clear your mind and refocus your energy. Another technique is progressive muscle relaxation, which involves tensing and slowly relaxing different muscle groups. This can reduce physical tension and promote mental calmness. Building a support network is also vital. Surround yourself with teammates, coaches, and family members who encourage and uplift you. A robust support system can provide comfort and advice when facing challenges.

Learning from failures and mistakes is another powerful way to build resilience. Instead of seeing mistakes as setbacks, view them as opportunities for growth. Reflect on what went wrong and how you can improve. This mindset shift can turn failures into valuable learning experiences. For instance, if you struck out in a crucial moment, analyze your swing, stance, and mental state. Use this information to make adjustments and come back stronger. Remember, every great player has faced failure. What sets them apart is their ability to learn and grow from these experiences.

Adversity plays a significant role in building resilience. When you face and overcome challenges, you become mentally tougher. Consider the story of a player who suffered a severe injury. The road to recovery was long and arduous, filled with physical therapy and setbacks. However, through sheer determination and mental strength, they returned to the field and performed better than ever. This experience taught them invaluable lessons about perseverance and resilience.

Similarly, recovering from performance slumps can build mental toughness. When you're in a slump, it can feel like you'll never get out. But you can turn things around by staying positive, working hard, and focusing on the process rather than the outcome. These experiences of overcoming adversity make you stronger and more resilient.

To practice mental resilience, try simulating high-pressure situations during practice. Create scenarios that mimic the stress and pressure of a real game. This can help you become more comfortable and confident in these situations. Another effective exercise is journaling and reflection. After each game or practice, write down your thoughts and experiences for a few minutes. Reflect on what went well and what didn't. This can help you process your emotions and learn from your experiences. Over time, these practices can significantly enhance your mental resilience.

I've consistently emphasized the importance of mental toughness with my players, especially when they're up against two strikes. In these situations, the key is to "battle" and stay strong. We focus on not giving in, getting beaten, and doing everything possible to avoid striking out. The goal is to stay in the at-bat as long as possible, showing grit and determination.

My coaching staff and I stress mental toughness in high-pressure moments, like when you're down to your last strike. We teach players to stay focused, let go of any previous mistakes, and keep a positive attitude. The main idea is to build confidence, stay persistent, and believe in yourself despite your challenges.

Building mental resilience is an ongoing process. It requires consistent practice and a willingness to learn from every experience, good or bad. By incorporating stress management techniques, building a support network, learning from failures, facing adversity, and practicing resilience exercises, you can develop the mental toughness needed to excel in baseball and life. The journey may be challenging, but the rewards are worth the effort.

The Role of Grit and Determination

Grit is the unsung hero of athletic success. The blend of passion and perseverance drives athletes to push through even the toughest challenges. In baseball, grit keeps players going when they're down in the count or have had a string of bad games. That inner fire says, "I will keep going no matter what." Grit involves long-term goal commitment, which means setting your sights on a distant target and relentlessly pursuing it despite the obstacles. This isn't just about raw talent; it's about the will to improve, the determination to keep practicing, and the passion for the game that fuels every effort.

Developing grit in athletes starts with setting and pursuing long-term goals. This means helping players see beyond the next game or season. Encourage them to consider where they want to be in five or ten years. What do they want to achieve in their baseball career? Once these long-term goals are set, break them down into smaller, actionable steps. This makes the big picture less daunting and provides a clear path forward. Another critical strategy is embracing and learning from challenges. Every setback is an opportunity to grow. When a player strikes out or makes an error, *instead of focusing on the failure, help them analyze what went wrong and how they can improve.* This shift in perspective can turn challenges into valuable learning experiences.

Consistency in effort and practice is another cornerstone of grit. It's not enough to work hard occasionally; grit requires sustained effort over time. Encourage players to develop a routine that includes regular, focused practice sessions. Consistency builds muscle memory, improves skills, and reinforces the mental toughness needed to persevere. It's the daily grind that often separates the good from the great. Remind your players that every practice, no matter how small, contributes to their long-term success. This consistent effort is what builds the foundation for achieving their goals.

Examples of gritty athletes in baseball are plentiful and inspiring. Consider the story of Mariano Rivera, who grew up in a small fishing village in Panama. Rivera faced numerous challenges on his path to becoming one of the greatest closers in baseball history. His journey was marked by determination and an unwavering commitment to his craft. Despite early career struggles and injuries, Rivera's grit and perseverance led him to achieve remarkable success, including five World Series championships and a record 652 career saves. His story is a testament to the power of grit in overcoming adversity and achieving greatness.

Another example is Max Scherzer, a pitcher known for his relentless work ethic and mental toughness. Scherzer faced several setbacks early in his career, including being traded and struggling with consistency. However, his determination to improve and his passion for the game never wavered. Scherzer's grit propelled him to become a three-time Cy Young Award winner and one of the most dominant pitchers in the modern era. His story illustrates how grit and perseverance can turn early struggles into long-term success.

Consider incorporating practical exercises into your training routine to build determination in your players. Goal-setting workshops can be incredibly effective. These sessions help players articulate their long-term goals and break them down into achievable steps. Encourage them to write down their goals and review them regularly. Reflection on personal motivations is another powerful tool. Ask your players to reflect on why they love the game and what drives them to succeed. This self-awareness can fuel their determination and keep them motivated during tough times. Incremental progress tracking is also valuable. Help your players track their progress over time, celebrating small victories. This boosts morale and reinforces the idea that consistent effort leads to improvement.

Working with one of the most talented kids I've ever coached in high school, despite his physical gifts, he often got discouraged after making a mistake and would worry about getting pulled from the game. This was partly because his previous coach had a habit of benching players who made errors. He had a hard time letting go of his mistakes. My goal was to build his grit and self-confidence. I worked with him to play without fear and to stay focused on each play. The key was to let go of what went wrong, move on, and concentrate on the next opportunity. As he started to experience success, his confidence grew. He became more determined and didn't want to disappoint his teammates or coaches. The team also made sure he knew they trusted him. His improvement was significant and inspiring.

As we wrap up this section, remember that grit isn't something you're born with; it's something you cultivate through passion, perseverance, and a relentless pursuit of your goals. *Encourage your players to embrace challenges, stay consistent in their efforts, and always keep their long-term goals in sight.* By fostering grit and determination, you'll help them succeed in baseball and equip them with the mental tools to face any challenge life throws their way.

2

FOCUS AND CONCENTRATION TECHNIQUES

We were up by two runs in the top of the last inning, with one out. The other team had runners on first and second, and my pitcher was feeling the pressure, especially after our second baseman made an error. I called time and went to the mound to talk to both of them. I told them to learn from the mistake but to move on and focus on the next play.

We just needed one good pitch in the right spot to get a ground ball to the second baseman or shortstop, and I had confidence we could turn a double play. They returned to their positions, and sure enough, the pitcher threw the perfect pitch. The batter hit a grounder to second base, and we turned the double play to get out of the inning. We ended up winning the game.

Staying Present: Mindfulness on the Field

Mindfulness is a term you might have heard, but what does it mean, especially in the context of baseball? Simply put, *mindfulness is the practice of being fully present in the moment and aware of your thoughts, feelings, and surroundings without judgment.* It's about focusing on what's happening right now rather than getting caught up in past mistakes or future worries. In baseball, this means concentrating on the pitch you're about to throw or the ball you're about to hit rather than dwelling on the last play or worrying about the game's outcome.

The science behind mindfulness is fascinating. Studies have shown that mindfulness can change the structure and function of the brain in ways that improve focus, reduce stress, and enhance performance. When you practice mindfulness, you activate areas of the brain associated with attention and emotional regulation. This can help you stay calm under pressure, make better decisions, and perform consistently at a high level. For athletes, this mental edge can be the difference between a good performance and a great one.

Mindfulness offers numerous benefits for athletes. One of the most significant is reduced anxiety and stress. When fully present, you're not worrying about past mistakes or future outcomes, which can help you stay calm and focused. This is crucial in high-pressure situations, where anxiety can quickly derail your performance. Mindfulness also improves concentration and decision-making. Training your mind to stay present can enhance your ability to focus on the task and make quick, effective decisions during the game. This can lead to better performance on the field and more consistent results.

Several mindfulness exercises are particularly effective for baseball players. One simple yet powerful technique is focused breathing. Take a moment to concentrate on your breath between pitches or during breaks. Inhale deeply, hold for a moment, and then exhale slowly. This can help calm your nerves and bring your attention back to the present moment. Another helpful exercise is the body scan meditation. Start at your toes and slowly move up to your head, paying attention to any sensations without judgment. This practice can help you stay grounded and aware of your body, which is crucial for maintaining focus during the game.

Focusing on your senses during gameplay is another effective mindfulness technique. Pay attention to the feel of the bat in your hands, the sound of the ball hitting the glove, or the sight of the pitcher's windup. Engaging your senses can anchor you in the present moment and enhance your overall awareness. These exercises might seem simple, but they can profoundly impact your performance. Consistent practice can help you develop the mental discipline to stay present and focused, even in high-pressure situations.

Professional athletes across various sports have successfully incorporated mindfulness into their routines. Kobe Bryant, for example, credited mindfulness and meditation for giving him a mental edge on the court. Similarly, Michael Jordan used mindfulness to stay focused and calm during games. Players like Sean Doolittle have embraced mindfulness practices to improve their performance in baseball. Doolittle, a relief pitcher, has talked about how mindfulness helps him stay present and focused, which is crucial for his role in high-stakes situations.

Several baseball teams have also integrated mindfulness training into their programs. The Chicago Cubs, under manager Joe Maddon, implemented mindfulness practices during their historic World Series run in 2016. The team worked with a mindfulness coach to develop techniques that helped players stay focused and calm under pressure. This holistic approach to mental training contributed to their success and demonstrated the power of mindfulness in sports.

To help you get started with mindfulness, here are a few exercises you can try:

Mindfulness Exercises for Baseball Players

1. Focused Breathing: Take a deep breath, hold it for a moment, and then exhale slowly. Repeat this several times, focusing solely on your breath. This can help calm

your nerves and bring your attention back to the present moment.

2. Body Scan Meditation: Sit or lie down comfortably. Start at your toes and slowly move up to your head, paying attention to any sensations without judgment. This practice can help you stay grounded and aware of your body.

3. Sensory Focus: During gameplay, pay attention to your senses. Feel the bat in your hands, hear the ball hitting the glove, and see the pitcher's windup. Engaging your senses can anchor you in the present moment and enhance your overall awareness.

These exercises are simple but powerful. With consistent practice, they can help you stay present, focused, and ready to perform at your best.

In-Game Focus Drills

Maintaining focus during a game is crucial for any baseball player. The ability to concentrate on the present moment, especially during high-pressure situations, can often be the difference between winning and losing. Focus drills are essential because they enhance situational awareness, improve reaction time, and sharpen decision-making skills. When you're on the field, distractions are everywhere —from the crowd's noise to the pressure of the game itself. Focus drills help you tune out these distractions and zero in on what's important: the next play.

For pitchers, focus drills can be as simple as counting breaths between pitches. This technique helps you stay calm and centered, especially when the game is on the line. You can block out external distractions and maintain a steady rhythm by focusing on your breath. Another effective drill for pitchers is visualizing the catcher's mitt as the only target. This narrows your focus and helps you deliver more accurate pitches.

Batters can benefit from tracking the ball from the pitcher's hand. This drill trains your eyes to pick up the ball's trajectory early, giving you more time to react. Another helpful exercise is to focus on the pitcher's release point. By honing in on this specific spot, you can better anticipate the type of pitch coming your way. These drills improve your hitting accuracy and boost your confidence at the plate.

Fielders, on the other hand, can practice visualizing different play scenarios. Imagine various situations before the ball is even hit —runners on base, potential double plays, or diving catches. This mental preparation helps you react more quickly and make smarter decisions during the game. Another effective drill is to focus on the ball's spin and trajectory during practice. This trains your eyes and enhances your ability to judge the ball's path, making you a more reliable fielder.

Integrating focus drills into your regular practice routine is critical to making them effective. Start with short, frequent focus sessions during training. These can be as brief as a few minutes but should be consistent. For instance, pitchers can practice their breathing exercises during bullpen sessions, while batters can work on tracking the ball during batting practice. Incorporate these drills into your warm-ups as well. A few minutes of focused breathing or visualization can set the tone for a productive practice.

Evaluating the effectiveness of focus drills is crucial for continuous improvement. One way to assess their impact is by tracking improvements in game situations. Keep a record of your performance before and after incorporating focus drills. Note any changes in your reaction time, decision-making, and overall game awareness. Player feedback is another valuable tool. Encourage players to self-assess and share their experiences with focus drills. This fosters a sense of accountability and provides insights into which drills are most effective.

For example, I once coached a team where we implemented a focus drill called "The Hitter's Eye." Before each pitch, the batter had to call out the type of pitch they expected based on the pitcher's hand position. Over time, this drill improved their pitch recognition and reaction time, leading to higher batting averages. The players also reported feeling more confident and less anxious at the plate, demonstrating the drill's effectiveness.

These drills are not one-size-fits-all. Tailor them to your specific needs and positions. The key is consistency and commitment. Over time, these focus drills will become second nature, helping you stay locked in during games.

Overcoming Distractions

Distractions are everywhere in baseball and can mess with your focus and performance if you let them. Think about the crowd noise, the constant chatter from the stands, and the unpredictable elements of the environment. These external distractions can easily pull your attention away from the game. Then, there are internal distractions, like negative self-talk and internal doubts. Have you ever replayed a mistake in your head or worried about what might go wrong? That's your mind working against you, not for you. And let's not forget about the psychological warfare from opponents, who might try to throw you off your game with their behavior or taunts. The pressure of the game itself can also be a huge distraction, especially in high-stakes situations.

To block out these external distractions, you need some solid strategies. One effective method is using earplugs or noise-canceling headphones during practice. This helps you get used to focusing despite the noise. Another great technique is developing a pre-pitch routine that keeps you centered. This could be as simple as adjusting your gloves, taking a deep breath, or repeating a calming phrase. These rituals can ground you and create a mental buffer against the chaos around you. The key is to make these routines consistent, so they become automatic and help you stay focused during the game.

Managing internal distractions and self-talk requires a different set of tools. Positive affirmation techniques work wonders here. Instead of letting negative thoughts spiral, replace them with positive, empowering statements. Tell yourself, "I've practiced for this," or "I've got the skills to handle this." Mindfulness meditation can also help clear your mind of clutter. Spend a few minutes each day practicing mindfulness to train your brain to stay present and focused. This way, when negative thoughts creep in, you can acknowledge them and then let them go, bringing your focus back to the game.

Real-life examples show how effective these strategies can be. Take, for instance, the routines of major league players like David Ortiz, who was known for his pre-bat rituals to stay focused. Ortiz would step out of the batter's box, adjust his batting gloves, and take a deep breath before each pitch. This routine helped him block out distractions and zero in on the task. Another example is pitcher Jon Lester, who has openly talked about using mindfulness techniques to manage his focus and stay calm under pressure. Lester's ability to block out heckling fans and maintain his composure on the mound is a testament to the power of these mental strategies.

The key to success in baseball is learning how to overcome distractions. Whether it's fans, the umpire, or the opposing team, staying focused on the moment is essential. Our job as players and coaches is to teach how to stay present, breathe, and focus on executing the next pitch. Remember, the opponent is just another team wearing different uniforms.

We don't worry about what the crowd says, or the umpire does. The only thing that matters is the next pitch. Breathe, execute the pitch, and then breathe again. Our goal is simple: win one pitch at a time.

Blocking out external and internal distractions is crucial for maintaining peak performance in baseball. Using tools like earplugs during practice, developing pre-pitch routines, practicing positive affirmations, and engaging in mindfulness meditation, you can train your mind to stay focused and present, no matter what's happening around you. These techniques not only improve your performance on the field but also give you the mental resilience to handle any challenge that comes your way.

Mental Reps: Practicing Focus Off the Field

Mental reps are a powerful tool that can significantly boost your performance on the field. Think of them as mental rehearsals where you visualize game scenarios and mentally practice plays. These mental reps are as important as physical practice because they help reinforce focus and readiness, even when you're not on the field. The concept is simple: by vividly imagining yourself in various game situations, you can prepare your mind for the real thing. This mental preparation can help you stay sharp, anticipate plays better, and execute with greater confidence.

To effectively conduct mental reps, you must set aside quiet time for visualization. Find a comfortable spot where you won't be disturbed. Close your eyes and start by taking a few deep breaths to calm your mind. Then, begin visualizing specific game scenarios. Picture yourself at bat, facing a tough pitcher. Imagine the pitch coming towards you, the sound of the ball hitting the bat, and the feeling of making solid contact. Use guided imagery to enhance your focus. The more detailed and vivid your visualization will be, the more effective it will be. You can even incorporate all your senses— smell the grass, hear the crowd, feel the ball in your hand. This makes the mental rehearsal more realistic and impactful.

The benefits of mental reps are numerous. One of the most significant is better anticipation of game situations. By mentally rehearsing different scenarios, you train your brain to recognize patterns and respond quickly. This can give you a split-second advantage, which is often all it takes to make a great play. Another benefit is increased confidence in executing plays. When you've already seen yourself succeed in your mind, you're more likely to perform well in reality. This mental preparation can also help reduce anxiety and calm you under pressure.

Professional athletes have long recognized the power of mental reps. Take, for instance, Michael Jordan, who famously used visualization to prepare for games. Jordan would spend time before each game picturing himself making key plays, which helped him stay focused and confident. In baseball, players like Derek Jeter have also used mental reps effectively. Jeter would visualize himself making clutch hits and defensive plays, contributing to his legendary consistency and performance under pressure. These athletes' routines highlight the importance of mental reps in achieving peak performance.

Studies have shown that mental reps can have a tangible impact on performance. One study involving basketball players found that those who practiced mental visualization alongside physical practice improved their free-throw shooting percentage more than those who only practiced physically. This demonstrates that mental reps can enhance physical skills and overall performance. Similar results have been observed in baseball. Players who incorporate mental reps into their training routines often report improved focus, better anticipation, and increased confidence.

There are two ways we do mental reps in our training routines. One example is when we're fielding ground balls. Let's say we have three players at shortstop, and we're hitting ground balls during practice. The first player fields the ball while the others behind him simulate the play mentally — they go through the motions without the ball. That's a mental rep.

Another way we get mental reps is when a batter is in the box, and the on-deck hitter also takes mental reps. The on-deck hitter times the pitcher and watches the pitches, acting like they're about to hit without actually swinging. Depending on how many pitches are thrown to the current batter, you can get anywhere from one to six mental reps before it's your turn to hit.

Mental reps are not a substitute for physical practice but a powerful complement. Setting aside time for visualization and guided imagery can reinforce your focus and readiness. This mental preparation can help you anticipate game situations better, execute plays with greater confidence, and stay calm under pressure. Whether you're a player looking to improve your performance or a coach wanting to inspire your team, incorporating mental reps into your training routine can make a significant difference.

Building a Pre-Game Mental Routine

Having a pre-game mental routine is crucial for any athlete. It sets the stage for your performance, helping to reduce pre-game anxiety and establish a consistent mental state. When you have a routine, you're not just winging it—you have a plan. This consistency can be a game-changer, especially when nerves creep in. Following a set routine creates a sense of familiarity and control, which can help calm your mind and prepare you for the task ahead.

Set specific goals for the game to build an effective pre-game mental routine. What do you want to achieve mentally during this game? Maybe it's staying focused through every pitch or maintaining a positive attitude regardless of the score. Write these goals down and revisit them before every game. Next, incorporate mindfulness and visualization exercises. Spend a few minutes visualizing yourself executing key plays flawlessly. Picture the ball leaving your hand or bat how you want it to. This mental rehearsal can make these actions feel more natural when you're in the game.

Establishing a consistent pre-game ritual is also essential. This could include specific activities like listening to a particular song, doing a series of stretches, or even repeating a motivational phrase to yourself. The key is to make these rituals consistent and become second nature. When game day comes, you'll find that these small, consistent actions help put you in the right frame of mind. It's like flipping a switch that tells your brain, "It's game time."

Many successful baseball players and teams have well-defined pre-game routines. Take Derek Jeter, for example. Before every game, Jeter had a specific set of actions he would go through, from the way he tied his shoes to the stretches he performed. This routine helped him get into the zone and perform consistently. Another great example is the Boston Red Sox, which has team rituals that involve specific warm-up exercises and mental prep sessions. These routines are about physical readiness and getting the mind in sync with the body.

Self-assessment after games is crucial for refining and improving your pre-game routine. Take a few minutes to reflect on how well your routine prepared you for the game. Were there parts that felt particularly effective? Were there elements that seemed unnecessary or distracting? Make notes and adjust accordingly. Seeking feedback from coaches and teammates can also provide valuable insights. They might notice things you don't, such as changes in your behavior or performance that correlate with your pre-game routine.

One of my players used to struggle with pre-game jitters. He'd get overwhelmed and lose focus right at the start of games. To help him, we built a pre-game routine that included deep breathing exercises, visualizing himself making successful plays and following a specific warm-up sequence. Over time, this routine helped him feel more calm and focused. His anxiety went down, and his performance improved significantly.

This showed me how powerful a solid pre-game mental routine can be. There's no one-size-fits-all approach, though. The key is to figure out what works best for you and stick to it.

Building a pre-game mental routine is about consistency and personalization. It's about finding the right combination of psychological and physical activities that prepare you for the game. By setting specific mental goals, incorporating mindfulness and visualization, and establishing consistent rituals, you can create a routine that helps you stay focused and perform at your best. Self-assessment and feedback will help you refine and improve this routine, making it an invaluable part of your game-day preparation.

In the next chapter, we'll explore emotional regulation strategies, exploring how to manage your emotions during high-stress situations to stay calm and collected on the field.

3
EMOTIONAL REGULATION
STRATEGIES

We were down by three runs in the bottom of the seventh, with the bases loaded and two outs, when the other team opted to make a pitching change. I took the opportunity to talk to our next batter and all three base runners. I explained the situation and told him what pitch to expect. "A fastball is coming—when it does, don't miss it. When you hit it, it's going off the right centerfield wall, and you are going to clear the bases. I instructed the runner at first base to get a great secondary lead and score.

Did I know for certain what pitch was coming? No! My experience taught me the other team was in trouble, and they were about to face the nine hole hitter. I assumed a fast ball was coming, but more important, I was trying to instill confidence that I had faith he could execute under duress. It was a testament to the power of staying calm under pressure and believing in oneself and one's teammates. Staying calm under pressure is crucial in baseball.

Staying Calm Under Pressure

Staying calm under pressure is crucial in baseball. It prevents rash decisions and enhances focus and clarity, allowing you to perform at your best. When relaxed, you can think, make better choices, and execute your skills more effectively. Panic, on the other hand, clouds your judgment and leads to mistakes. Imagine being on the pitcher's mound with the game on the line. If you let the pressure get to you, you're more likely to throw a wild pitch or make a poor decision. But if you remain calm, you can focus on the catcher's mitt and deliver a strike.

One technique to stay calm during high-stress moments is visualization of successful outcomes. Before you step onto the field, take a few moments to visualize yourself making successful plays. Picture the ball leaving your bat or your hand, and see it going exactly where you want it to go. This mental rehearsal can create a sense of familiarity and confidence, reducing anxiety and helping you stay calm when it matters most. Another effective strategy is to develop pre-performance routines. These routines, whether they involve adjusting your gloves, taking a deep breath, or repeating a calming phrase, can ground you and create a sense of control and consistency.

Experience also plays a significant role in staying calm under pressure. The more you expose yourself to high-pressure situations, the more accustomed you become to handling them. Gradual exposure techniques like participating in high-stakes practice games or simulated pressure scenarios can help you build composure over time. By gradually increasing the intensity of these situations, you can train your mind and body to remain calm and focused. Simulation of game-like pressure in practice, where you recreate the conditions of a high-stakes game, can also be highly effective. This prepares you mentally and physically for the real thing, making the actual game feel less intimidating.

Let's look at some examples of athletes who excelled by staying calm under pressure. Mariano Rivera, one of the greatest closers in baseball history, was known for his composure on the mound. In the 2003 American League Championship Series, Rivera pitched three scoreless innings in Game 7, helping the Yankees secure a trip to the World Series. His calm demeanor and focus under immense pressure were critical to his success. Another example is Derek Jeter, who consistently performed in clutch situations. Jeter's ability to stay calm and focused, even in the most high-pressure moments, made him a reliable and effective player throughout his career.

Visualizing Success Exercise

- Find a Quiet Space: Sit comfortably and close your eyes. Take a few deep breaths to center yourself.
- Imagine a Successful Outcome: Picture yourself in a high-pressure situation. See yourself executing the play flawlessly. Engage all your senses—feel the bat in your hands, hear the crowd, see the ball.
- Repeat Daily: Spend a few minutes each day visualizing successful outcomes. Consistency is critical to making this technique effective.

These strategies and examples show that staying calm under pressure is not just about innate talent; it's about preparation, practice, and mental conditioning. By incorporating visualization, establishing pre-performance routines, and gradually exposing yourself to high-pressure situations, you can develop the composure needed to excel in baseball and beyond.

Effective Breathing Techniques

Breathing exercises are an underrated yet powerful tool in emotional regulation. The connection between your breath and your emotional state is profound. When you're anxious or stressed, your breathing becomes shallow and rapid, sending signals to your brain that you're in danger. On the other hand, slow, deep breaths can calm your nervous system, reduce stress, and bring clarity to your mind. The scientific basis for breathing techniques lies in their ability to activate the parasympathetic nervous system, which counteracts the fight-or-flight response. Imagine being on the field, heart racing, nerves on edge. Deep breaths can help reset your body and mind, allowing you to focus and perform your best.

To start, let's go through some specific breathing exercises. Diaphragmatic breathing is a fundamental technique. Sit or lie down comfortably. Place one hand on your chest and the other on your abdomen. Inhale deeply through your nose, letting your abdomen rise while keeping your chest still. Exhale slowly through your mouth, feeling your abdomen fall. Repeat this for a few minutes. The 4-7-8 breathing technique is another effective method. Inhale quietly through your nose for a count of four, hold your breath for seven, and exhale completely through your mouth for a count of eight. This exercise can quickly calm your mind. Lastly, there's the box breathing method. Inhale through your nose for a count of four, hold your breath for a count of four, exhale through your mouth for a count of four, and hold your breath again for a count of four. This simple yet powerful technique helps stabilize your breathing rhythm and reduce stress.

Timing and integration of these breathing exercises are crucial. During game breaks, take a moment to practice diaphragmatic breathing. This can help you stay calm and focused between innings or during timeouts. Incorporate the 4-7-8 breathing technique into your pre-performance routines. Before stepping onto the field, spend a few minutes practicing this method to center yourself and reduce anxiety. In moments of high stress, such as when you're at bat or on the mound in a tight situation, use box breathing to regain control and maintain composure. These exercises can seamlessly integrate into your routine, providing instant relief and focus when needed.

Athletes across various sports have successfully used breathing techniques to enhance their performance. Michael Phelps, the legendary swimmer, practiced deep breathing before every race to calm his mind and prepare for the challenge ahead. Similarly, LeBron James uses breathing exercises as part of his pre-game routine to stay focused and relaxed. In baseball, players like Alex Rodriguez have credited breathing techniques for helping them stay calm and perform under pressure. These athletes' experiences highlight the effectiveness of proper breathing in managing stress and improving performance.

One of my players used to let his nerves get the best of him during critical moments. To help him, we introduced deep breathing into his routine. Before every game, he spent a few minutes practicing it. Over time, he noticed a big difference in how calm and focused he felt, and his performance on the field improved. He became more confident in high-pressure situations, showing how powerful breathing techniques can be for emotional control and performance.

We teach our players to breathe from the diaphragm between each pitch. Whether you're a pitcher aiming for a strike or a batter visualizing the perfect hit, you take a deep breath and focus on executing the next pitch. It's all about staying in the moment. The process is simple but effective: we don't worry about what's already happened or what's coming in the next few pitches. All we can do is breathe, focus, and win one pitch or one at-bat swing at a time.

Incorporating breathing exercises into your routine doesn't require much time but offers immense benefits. Whether you're a player looking to improve your game or a coach wanting to help your team, these techniques can make a significant difference. Start with simple exercises like diaphragmatic breathing and gradually incorporate more advanced methods like the 4-7-8 technique and box breathing. Practice them regularly, integrate them into your game breaks and pre-performance routines, and use them in moments of high stress. The results will speak for themselves, helping you stay calm, focused, and ready to perform at your best.

Breathing Techniques Checklist

- Diaphragmatic Breathing: Practice for a few minutes daily to improve overall relaxation and focus.
- 4-7-8 Breathing Technique: Use before games to reduce anxiety and center yourself.
- Box Breathing Method: Integrate during high-stress moments to regain control and maintain composure.

These breathing techniques are simple yet highly effective. By making them a regular part of your routine, you can enhance your emotional regulation, reduce stress, and improve your overall performance on the field.

Using Positive Self-Talk

Positive self-talk is potent in maintaining a positive mindset and enhancing performance. Think of it as the internal dialogue that goes on in your head. It's the voice that either lifts you or brings you down. Positive self-talk is about encouraging yourself, focusing on your strengths, and believing in your abilities. On the flip side, negative self-talk can be detrimental. The voice says, "You can't do this," or "You're going to mess up." This kind of thinking can sap your confidence and negatively impact your performance. Studies have shown that athletes who engage in positive self-talk perform better, have higher confidence levels, and manage stress more effectively.

To cultivate effective positive self-talk, start by creating personal mantras. These are short, powerful phrases that you can repeat to yourself to build confidence and focus. For example, "I am prepared" or "I can handle this." These mantras serve as mental anchors, helping you stay grounded and positive. Another technique is to reframe negative thoughts. When you catch yourself thinking negatively, flip the script. Instead of saying, "I always strike out," tell yourself, "I'll learn from this and get better." Using affirmations is also crucial. Affirmations are positive statements that reinforce your goals and abilities. Repeating affirmations like, "I am a strong hitter," or "I perform well under pressure" can help shift your mindset from doubt to confidence.

Practicing positive self-talk requires consistency. One effective exercise is keeping a daily affirmation journal. Each day, write down positive statements about yourself and your abilities. This practice can help reinforce a positive mindset and make positive self-talk a habit. Combining visualization with positive self-talk can also be powerful. As you visualize successful outcomes, incorporate positive affirmations. For instance, while visualizing a perfect swing, repeat to yourself, "I hit the ball with power and precision." Role-playing scenarios can further reinforce positive self-talk. Practice different game situations with a focus on maintaining positive dialogue. This can help you stay positive and confident in real-game scenarios.

Athletes who successfully use positive self-talk often stand out for their mental resilience. Take Michael Jordan, for example. Known for his mental toughness, Jordan frequently used positive self-talk to stay focused and confident, especially during high-pressure moments. His mantra, "I've missed more than 9,000 shots in my career. I've lost almost 300 games. I've failed over and over and over again in my life. And that is why I succeed," highlights his ability to reframe failure as a stepping stone to success. Another example is Serena Williams, who uses positive affirmations to boost her confidence before matches. Her consistent use of positive self-talk has played a significant role in her dominance in tennis.

Positive self-talk is crucial in baseball, especially when the pressure is on. It's not just about what players say out loud but what they tell themselves and how they carry themselves on the field. I remember we had a pitcher who started to struggle—you could see it in his body language. He wasn't saying he couldn't handle the moment, but his negative self-talk showed how he moved.

When that happens, I remind them that we believe in their ability to execute. And if they don't get it right this time, it's not the end of the world. No one's life is on the line, and the game isn't over. The key is to forget the mistake, let it go, flush it, and be ready to come back and execute again.

Our team has a saying: "There's always a chance to make something good happen." We have confidence in each player and know everyone is in the right position now.

Positive self-talk is a game-changer. You can cultivate a positive mindset by creating personal mantras, reframing negative thoughts, and using affirmations. To reinforce these habits, practice exercises like daily affirmation journals, visualization combined with self-talk, and role-playing scenarios. The experiences of athletes like Michael Jordan and Serena Williams and my players demonstrate the transformative power of positive self-talk. Embrace this tool to boost your confidence, manage stress, and enhance your performance on and off the field.

Handling Negative Emotions

Negative emotions are part and parcel of sports, and baseball is no exception. Athletes often grapple with frustration, anger, fear, and disappointment. Imagine striking out with the bases loaded or making an error that costs your team the game. The frustration can be overwhelming, leading to anger that clouds your judgment. Fear might creep in during high-stakes moments, making you second-guess your abilities. Disappointment lingers after a loss or a poor performance, sapping your motivation. These emotions impact your concentration and performance, making it crucial to manage them effectively.

One effective way to handle negative emotions is through emotional labeling. This involves identifying and naming your feelings as they arise. For example, if you're frustrated, acknowledge it by saying, "I'm frustrated because I missed that play." This simple act of labeling can help you gain control over your emotions and reduce their intensity. Cognitive reframing is another powerful technique. This means changing the way you think about a situation. Instead of viewing a mistake as a failure, see it as a learning opportunity. For instance, if you struck out, reframe it by saying, "This is a chance to learn and improve my swing." Physical activity can also help release built-up tension. A quick run, push-ups, or even a few minutes of stretching can help dissipate negative energy and clear your mind.

Support systems play a vital role in managing emotions. Open communication channels with your coaches, teammates, and family can provide a much-needed outlet for your feelings. Coaches can offer valuable feedback and advice, helping you navigate challenging times. Teammates who understand what you're going through can provide support and solidarity. Family members can offer comfort and perspective, reminding you that it's just a game and not the end of the world. Seeking feedback is also essential. Constructive criticism can guide you on how to improve, while positive reinforcement can boost your confidence.

I had an outfielder who was super competitive and talented and played hard every game but was always his own harshest critic. No matter what we said or did, he was hard on himself. So, at practice, we decided to let him have his moment. We gave him the space to react, but we set a limit —he had 30 seconds to sit in the dugout, scream into his glove, talk to himself, or sit there and cool off.

After those 30 seconds, he had to talk to a coach, acknowledge that he was good, let the past go, and be ready to move on. That way, he could release the frustration and refocus without affecting his game.

Physical activity also played a significant role in managing emotions for another player, Mike. After particularly tough games, Mike would go for a run or hit the gym. This physical release helped him manage his frustration and clear his mind. He found that by channeling his negative energy into physical activity, he could return to the game with a clearer head and a more positive attitude.

Athletes who successfully manage negative emotions often experience turnaround moments. Take the case of Alex Rodriguez, who faced immense pressure and criticism throughout his career. Despite this, Rodriguez learned to handle his emotions effectively, often seeking advice from mentors and staying focused on his goals. His ability to manage negative emotions was crucial to his successful career.

Handling negative emotions is a skill that can be developed with practice and the right strategies. Emotional labeling, cognitive reframing, physical activity, and robust support systems are vital techniques for managing emotions effectively. By implementing these strategies, you can maintain focus, improve your performance, and navigate baseball's emotional ups and downs with greater resilience.

Emotional Recovery After Mistakes

Recovering quickly from mistakes is a fundamental skill in baseball. When you make an error, it's easy to let it spiral into a series of poor plays, affecting your overall performance. Swift emotional recovery helps you maintain your performance and prevents a negative spiral. Imagine making a critical error in the field. If you dwell on it, you might miss the next play or make another mistake. But if you recover quickly, you can refocus and move on, minimizing the impact of the error on your game.

One effective technique for quick emotional recovery is immediate refocusing. When you make a mistake, shift your focus to the present moment. Concentrate on the next play, the next pitch, or the next at-bat. This helps you stay grounded and prevents your mind from dwelling on the error. Another strategy is mindfulness and grounding exercises. Take a deep breath, feel your feet on the ground, and center yourself. This can help you regain composure and stay focused on the game.

Learning from mistakes without dwelling on them is crucial. Reflect on what went wrong and how you can improve, but don't let it consume you. For instance, if you struck out, analyze your swing, stance, and mental state. Use this information to make adjustments, but then move on. Dwelling on mistakes only amplifies their negative impact. Instead, use them as learning opportunities to build resilience.

Reflective journaling on errors can be a powerful tool for emotional recovery. After each game, take a few minutes to write down your mistakes and reflect on what you learned from them. This practice helps you process your emotions and identify areas for improvement. Setting improvement goals is another effective strategy. After reflecting on your mistakes, set specific, achievable goals to address them. For example, if you struggled with your swing, set a goal to work on your technique during the next practice. This proactive approach helps you focus on improvement rather than on past errors.

Let's consider some examples of athletes who have mastered quick emotional recovery. One such player is Ichiro Suzuki, known for his incredible focus and resilience. Ichiro had a unique ability to bounce back from mistakes quickly. After making a rare fielding error in one game, he immediately refocused and made a spectacular catch in the next inning. His ability to recover rapidly and stay composed was crucial to his long and successful career.

Another example is Clayton Kershaw, a pitcher who has faced challenges. In the 2016 playoffs, Kershaw gave up a crucial home run that could have demoralized him. Instead, he refocused, adjusted his strategy, and pitched several scoreless innings, helping his team secure the win. Kershaw's ability to learn from his mistakes without dwelling on them has made him one of the most resilient pitchers in the game.

When a player makes a mistake, you can help them refocus and move on to the next pitch, at-bat, or play on the field. You've got to keep reminding them to let it go and focus on what's next. They need to "flush it" and move on, and their body language should show that they're ready for the next play. Dwelling on mistakes won't help—staying in the moment and refocusing will.

Everyone makes errors but must trust that their teammates will have their back. That's all you can do—help them stay locked in and ready to go again.

Emotional recovery from mistakes is about maintaining focus, learning from errors, and building resilience. Techniques like immediate refocusing, mindfulness exercises, reflective journaling, and setting improvement goals can help you bounce back quickly and stay in the game. The stories of players like Ichiro Suzuki, Clayton Kershaw, Alex, and Emily illustrate that you can turn mistakes into opportunities for growth and success with the right strategies.

4
CONFIDENCE BUILDING

B uilding confidence is about showing your team that you genuinely believe in them. I remember one game where our pitcher was in trouble—the first three batters from the other team got on base, and we were trying to protect a lead. You could see his frustration in his slumped shoulders and poor body language.

I went to the mound and told him the coaching staff believed in him. We knew he could throw just a handful of good pitches to get us out of the inning and back into the dugout. He had practiced hard, was talented, and everyone trusted him. We just needed him to minimize the damage to one run.

And that's precisely what he did. He gave up a sacrifice fly, which allowed one run to score but then got the next batter to ground into a double play. That boosted his confidence, and he struck out the next hitter to end the inning. It was a great example of how belief and trust can help players turn things around.

Setting Realistic Goals

Goal setting is crucial for building confidence in athletes. When you set and achieve goals, it boosts your self-belief and motivation. It's like laying down stepping stones that lead you toward your bigger dreams. Achieving these goals builds confidence and provides a sense of accomplishment and progress. On the other hand, unrealistic goals can be discouraging. Setting the bar too high and failing to reach it can lead to frustration and self-doubt. That's why it's essential to set realistic, achievable goals that push you just enough to grow without overwhelming you.

To create practical goals, you can use the SMART criteria. SMART stands for Specific, Measurable, Attainable, Relevant, and Time-bound. Start by defining specific actions or outcomes you want to achieve. For example, instead of saying, "I want to improve my batting," specify, "I want to increase my batting average by 10 points." This makes your goal clear and focused. Next, make sure your goal is measurable. This means you need a way to track your progress. For instance, you can measure your batting average over a month. The goal should also be attainable. Set goals that challenge you but are still within your reach. Aiming to increase your batting average by 10 points is realistic, while aiming for 50 points might be too much. Relevance is also significant. Your goals should align with your overall objectives and be meaningful to you. Lastly, make sure your goals are time-bound. Set a deadline for achieving your goal, such as "by the end of the season" or "within the next three months." This adds a sense of urgency and helps you stay focused.

Breaking down long-term goals into short-term, actionable steps is essential for maintaining motivation and tracking progress. For example, if your long-term goal is to improve your batting average by 10 points by the end of the season, break it down into smaller steps. Start with a goal to improve your swing mechanics in the first month. Then, focus on increasing your contact rate in the second month. You can progress steadily without feeling overwhelmed by dividing your goal into manageable steps. This approach also allows you to celebrate small victories along the way, which further boosts your confidence.

Involving players in the goal-setting process is crucial for their commitment and motivation. Encourage self-assessment and reflection. Ask players to identify their strengths and areas for improvement. This self-awareness helps them set meaningful and relevant goals. Collaborative goal-setting sessions with coaches can also be highly effective. Sit down with your players and discuss their goals together. Offer guidance and support, but let them take ownership of their goals. Players are more likely to stay committed and motivated when they feel involved.

Monitoring and adjusting goals is an ongoing process. Regular check-ins and progress reviews are essential for staying on track. Schedule periodic meetings with your players to discuss their progress. Celebrate their achievements and provide constructive feedback on areas where they can improve. Flexibility in modifying goals based on performance is also essential. If a player needs help to meet a goal, work with them to adjust it. Sometimes, unforeseen challenges can arise, and it's necessary to adapt. This doesn't mean lowering your standards but being realistic and supportive in helping players achieve their best.

Goal Setting Worksheet

- Specific Goal: Define a clear and specific goal you want to achieve.
- Measurable: Determine how you will measure your progress.
- Attainable: Ensure your goal is challenging yet achievable.
- Relevant: Align your goal with your overall objectives.
- Time-bound: Set a deadline for achieving your goal.
- Short-Term Steps: Break down your goal into smaller, actionable steps.
- Check-ins: Schedule regular progress reviews.

Setting realistic goals is a powerful technique for building confidence in athletes. By using the SMART criteria, breaking down long-term goals into short-term steps, involving players in the process, and regularly monitoring and adjusting goals, you can help your players achieve success and maintain their motivation. This approach not only improves performance on the field but also fosters a positive and confident mindset that can benefit them in all areas of life.

Daily Affirmations for Athletes

Daily affirmations are a powerful tool for building confidence and shaping a positive mindset. At their core, affirmations are positive statements you repeat to yourself, designed to challenge and overcome self-sabotaging and negative thoughts. They are rooted in the belief that your thoughts can influence your reality. Psychologically, affirmations rewire your brain's neural pathways, helping you foster a more positive outlook. This is especially crucial in sports, where mental toughness is just as important as physical skill. Repeating affirmations can boost your confidence, reduce anxiety, and prepare you mentally for the challenges ahead.

Creating personalized affirmations involves introspection. Start by identifying your strengths and areas for improvement. Reflect on what you're good at and where you need more confidence. For example, if you're a great fielder but struggle at the plate, craft affirmations that reinforce your strengths while addressing your weaknesses. Write these affirmations in the present tense to make them more impactful. Use statements like, "I am improving my batting skills every day," or "I am a reliable and confident fielder." The present tense makes these statements feel more immediate and real, helping you internalize them more effectively.

Incorporating affirmations into your daily routine can make them a seamless part of your life. One practical way to do this is by establishing morning and evening rituals. Start your day by repeating your affirmations out loud or writing them down. This sets a positive tone for the day ahead. Similarly, end your day by reflecting on your affirmations and reinforcing those positive thoughts before you sleep. Visual reminders can also be incredibly effective. Use sticky notes on your mirror or change your phone wallpaper to display your affirmations. These constant visual cues help keep your mind focused on positive thoughts throughout the day.

Here are some powerful affirmations you can use to boost your confidence and mental toughness:

- "I am capable of achieving my goals."
- "I remain calm and focused under pressure."
- "I am a valuable and integral part of my team."

These statements might seem simple, but their impact can be profound. They constantly remind you of your abilities and potential, helping you stay motivated and focused on your goals.

Sometimes, we have pitchers going into high-pressure games, and in the days leading up, I reinforce one thing: there's nobody better for the job, and there's no one else I'd rather have on the mound. They've worked hard and earned the right to be in that spot. I remind them that they're more formidable than the other team, and that's why they're the ones who get the ball when it counts.

Affirmations are more than just positive statements; they are tools for mental training. You can harness their full potential by identifying your strengths and areas for improvement, writing affirmations in the present tense, and incorporating them into your daily routine. Constant reinforcement through morning and evening rituals and visual reminders helps solidify these positive thoughts in your mind. Ben and Lisa's examples show how affirmations can transform your mindset and performance, making them an invaluable part of your mental game strategy.

. . .

Learning from Failure

Failure is often viewed as the enemy in sports, but what if I told you it could be your most excellent teacher? Shifting the perception of failure from negative to positive is critical to building resilience and confidence. When you start seeing failure as a step toward success, you understand that every setback is an opportunity for growth and development. This mindset helps you focus on what you can learn from each experience rather than dwelling on the disappointment. It's about embracing the improvement process and recognizing that failure is not the end but a valuable part of the journey to success.

Analyzing and learning from mistakes is a crucial skill for any athlete. One effective method is post-game reflection sessions. After each game, take some time to reflect on what went wrong and why. This could be done individually or as a team. Discuss the mistakes openly and constructively, focusing on what can be learned rather than assigning blame. Keeping a failure journal can also be incredibly beneficial. Document each mistake and the lesson learned from it. Over time, you'll start to see patterns and areas for improvement. This practice helps you learn from your errors and reminds you of your growth and progress.

Building resilience through failure strengthens your mental toughness and confidence. Famous athletes have often turned their failures into stepping stones for success. Michael Jordan, for example, was cut from his high school basketball team, but he used that failure as motivation to become one of the greatest players of all time. Similarly, baseball legend Babe Ruth struck out more than most players in history but also hit more home runs. These stories emphasize the importance of perseverance and determination. Encouraging a mindset of perseverance means teaching players to keep pushing forward, even when things get tough. It's about developing a "never give up" attitude that helps them bounce back stronger after each setback.

Support systems play a crucial role in helping players cope with fail-

ure. As a coach, your feedback can make a significant difference. Giving constructive feedback helps players understand what went wrong and how to improve. Creating a supportive and non-judgmental environment is essential where players feel safe to make mistakes and learn from them. Encourage open communication and teamwork. When players know their coaches, teammates, and family support them, they're more likely to take risks and push themselves, knowing that failure is just a part of the learning process.

When a player fails—and everyone will at some point—they can't be afraid of failure because that's how we learn. You've got to let them play and let them play freely. After the game, the key is to determine if the mistake was physical or mental.

If it was physical, you already know what happened. But if it was a mental or emotional mistake, ask what they were thinking and how to avoid it next time. Everybody makes errors, but it's about understanding what went wrong and developing a plan to minimize the negative impact so it doesn't happen again.

Learning from failure is not just about analyzing mistakes; it's about building a mindset of resilience and perseverance. By redefining failure as a learning opportunity, utilizing techniques like post-game reflection and failure journals, and fostering a supportive environment, you can help your players develop the mental toughness needed to succeed. These stories illustrate the transformative power of this approach. Failure is not the end; it's a crucial part of the journey to success.

Celebrating Small Wins

Recognizing small achievements is vital for building confidence in athletes. These seemingly minor milestones can significantly boost morale and motivation, reinforcing the positive behaviors and habits that lead to long-term success. Celebrating small wins reminds players that every step forward is valuable, no matter how small it may seem. This approach helps maintain a positive atmosphere within the team, where progress is acknowledged and appreciated. Celebrating these minor accomplishments also encourages players to stay committed to their goals, knowing their hard work is being noticed and rewarded.

There are several practical ways to celebrate small wins. Verbal praise and positive reinforcement are among the simplest yet most effective methods. Acknowledging a player's effort or improvement with a few encouraging words can make a big difference in their confidence. For instance, saying, "Great job on that catch!" or "I noticed your swing is getting better!" can boost a player's self-esteem and motivation. Team recognition rituals can also be highly impactful, such as awarding game balls or giving shout-outs during team meetings. These rituals create a sense of camaraderie and reinforce the idea that every contribution is valuable. Personal rewards and incentives, like a player of the week award or a small token of appreciation, can further motivate players to strive for improvement.

Tracking progress through small wins is essential for building upon these successes. Progress charts and visual trackers can help players see their achievements over time, providing a tangible representation of their growth. These tools can be as simple as a chart on the wall or a digital tracker that players can update regularly. Reflecting on achievements during team meetings is another effective strategy. Take a few minutes during each meeting to highlight individual and team accomplishments. This practice boosts morale and fosters a culture of continuous improvement.

Successful baseball teams often have effective celebration practices that keep their players motivated. For example, some teams have a tradition of awarding a game ball to the player who made the most significant impact during the game. This simple gesture acknowledges the player's contribution and encourages others to step up. Another effective practice is holding end-of-week or end-of-month reflection sessions, where players and coaches discuss progress and celebrate achievements, no matter how small. These sessions can be an excellent opportunity to reinforce positive behaviors and set new goals.

One thing we focus on as a team is recognizing that winning is hard, so we celebrate our wins. Whenever we win a game, whether on the road or at home, I gather the team for a group picture, which we post on social media. It's a way to acknowledge our hard work and enjoy the moment together.

While we don't typically celebrate individual performances the same way, we have some fun props in the dugout. When a player hits a home run, he gets to wear a unique hat, and if he scores a run, we have a gold chain he can put on. But our main celebration is for the team to win. We take a picture with the scoreboard in the background, wherever we are, and post it with a reminder that winning is hard, and we're proud to celebrate it when it happens.

Players and coaches often testify to the positive impact of celebrating small wins. Players have shared how receiving a game ball for a crucial play boosted their confidence and motivated them to keep improving. Other coaches mentioned how team recognition rituals helped create a positive and supportive environment where players felt valued and appreciated. These testimonials highlight the importance of acknowledging and celebrating small achievements in building confidence and fostering a positive team culture.

Recognizing small achievements is a powerful tool for building confidence in athletes. Methods like verbal praise, team recognition rituals, personal rewards, and progress tracking can create a positive and motivating environment. Real-life examples and testimonials from players and coaches further emphasize the effectiveness of these practices. Celebrating small wins boosts morale and motivation and reinforces the positive behaviors and habits that lead to long-term success.

Role Models and Mentorship

Role models play a crucial role in building confidence among young athletes. When players see someone they admire achieving great things, it inspires them to believe in their potential. Positive role models can shape behavior and mindset, showing players what is possible through hard work and determination. For example, players like Derek Jeter and Jackie Robinson have become role models for their skills on the field, character, and perseverance. Their stories of overcoming obstacles and achieving greatness are potent motivators for aspiring athletes. When young players look up to a role model, they often adopt similar attitudes and work ethics, striving to emulate their success.

Finding and connecting with mentors can be a game-changer for young athletes. A good mentor should be knowledgeable, approachable, and genuinely interested in the mentee's development. Mentors should also be good listeners, offering guidance and support without being overbearing. Connecting with a potential mentor starts with identifying someone who embodies these qualities. Approach them with respect and a genuine interest in learning from their experiences. Be honest about your goals and challenges, and express how their mentorship could benefit you. Building a mentorship relationship takes time and effort, but the rewards are well worth it.

The benefits of mentorship for young athletes are immense. A mentor provides personalized guidance and support, helping you navigate the ups and downs of your athletic journey. They can share insights from their experiences, offering practical advice and encouragement. Mentors can also help you set realistic goals and develop strategies. Beyond the technical aspects of the sport, a mentor can provide life lessons, teaching you about resilience, discipline, and the importance of a positive attitude. A mentor and mentee relationship often goes beyond the field, impacting your personal development and growth.

Many athletes have thrived under the guidance of mentors. Take, for instance, the relationship between Tony Gwynn and Ted Williams. Gwynn, one of the greatest hitters in baseball history, often sought advice from Williams, a legendary figure in the sport. Williams' mentorship helped Gwynn refine his skills and approach to the game, contributing to his success. Another example is the mentorship between Kobe Bryant and Michael Jordan. Bryant often spoke about how Jordan's guidance helped shape his mindset and approach to basketball, leading to his illustrious career. These examples highlight the transformative power of mentorship in sports.

On my teams, our coaches were always mentors to their players. I've had the opportunity to mentor many players throughout their early careers, helping them grow both on and off the field.

Role models and mentors are invaluable in building confidence and guiding young athletes. Players can gain the inspiration, guidance, and support they need to succeed by looking up to positive role models and finding supportive mentors. The benefits of mentorship extend beyond the field, impacting personal growth and development. Let's continue to foster these relationships, knowing they can make a lasting difference in the lives of young athletes. In the next chapter, we'll explore advanced mental strategies for high school athletes, diving into techniques to take your mental game to the next level.

5
PARENTAL SUPPORT AND INVOLVEMENT

W hen coaching youth baseball many years ago, I had a player whose performance was inconsistent. One day, he'd get on base; the next, he'd strike out three times in a row. I noticed his parents were always in the stands, cheering loudly when he did well but visibly disappointed when he didn't. One evening after practice, I talked with his parents and suggested a shift in their approach. I asked them to focus on their son's effort rather than the outcome. They started praising him for his hard work and perseverance, regardless of the game's result. Over time, this player's confidence soared, and his performance stabilized. This experience underscored how crucial a positive home environment is for a young athlete's mental and emotional well-being.

I'd also suggest keeping it positive. Avoid shouting negative comments or giving technical advice during the game. That kind of pressure can weigh on players. Instead, we encourage parents to focus on support—at games, practices, or at home. Their encouragement means a lot!"

Creating a Positive Environment at Home

A supportive home atmosphere is foundational for a child's

mental development. When children feel supported and understood at home, their self-esteem and confidence naturally blossom. A positive home environment is a safe space where children can express their emotions, share their successes, and discuss their failures without fear of judgment. This emotional safety net fosters a sense of self-worth and resilience. When children know they are valued for who they are, not just for their accomplishments, they develop a healthier self-image and greater emotional well-being.

Open communication is vital to creating this nurturing environment. Encourage your child to talk about their day, feelings, and experiences on and off the field. Listen actively and validate their emotions, showing that you genuinely care about what they say. Establishing routines that include downtime and family activities can also create a sense of stability and connection. Simple acts like having dinner together, playing a board game, or walking can strengthen family bonds and provide a much-needed break from the pressures of sports and academics.

Another powerful strategy is rewarding effort rather than just results. Acknowledging your child's hard work and dedication to their sport reinforces positive behaviors and intrinsic motivation. Celebrate small victories and improvements instead of focusing solely on wins and losses. For instance, praise your child for their persistence in practice, teamwork, or sportsmanship. This approach helps them understand that their value isn't tied to their performance, reducing the pressure to achieve and fostering a love for the game.

Minimizing stressors at home is equally important. Avoid overscheduling your child's activities, as this can lead to burnout and increased anxiety. Ensure they have enough free time to relax, play, and pursue other interests. Creating a calm and organized living space can also create a more peaceful home environment. A clutter-free and well-organized home can reduce feelings of overwhelm and help your child feel more in control.

Parental behavior sets a powerful example for children. Demonstrating positive coping mechanisms when faced with stress or disappointment teaches your child how to handle their emotions constructively. Show them that it's okay to feel upset, but also model healthy ways to process and move past those feelings. Additionally, showing appreciation for effort and progress, rather than just outcomes, reinforces the idea that growth and learning are valuable in their own right.

I remember another player, Mia, whose parents were incredibly supportive. They always emphasized the importance of effort and personal growth over winning. When Mia had a challenging game, they would focus on the positives, like her hustle on the field or her teamwork. This approach helped Mia develop a resilient mindset and love for the game. She knew her parents valued her hard work and dedication, boosting her confidence and motivation.

Creating a positive environment at home is about more than just cheering from the sidelines. It's about fostering open communication, establishing supportive routines, and rewarding effort over results. It's about minimizing stress and setting a positive example through your behavior. Doing so can help your child develop the self-esteem, confidence, and emotional resilience they need to succeed on and off the field.

Reflection Section

- Open Communication: How can you encourage more open conversations with your child about their feelings and experiences?
- Rewarding Effort: Think of three ways to celebrate your child's effort and dedication, regardless of the outcome.
- Reducing Stress: Identify one or two activities you can remove from your child's schedule to give them more downtime.

- Positive Example: Reflect on how you handle stress and disappointment. What positive coping mechanisms can you model for your child?

Encouraging Without Pressuring

Knowing the difference between encouragement and pressure can affect your child's athletic experience. Encouragement is about motivating your child, helping them believe in themselves, and fostering a love for the game. Conversely, pressure can lead to anxiety, burnout, and losing interest in the sport. Signs of undue pressure might include your child expressing a fear of disappointing you, showing signs of stress before games, or even losing their love for baseball. On the flip side, positive encouragement boosts their self-esteem and helps them enjoy the sport more, creating a healthy environment for growth.

To encourage effectively, start by setting realistic expectations. Understand that not every game will be a home run, and not every practice will be perfect. What matters is the effort and improvement over time. Offer constructive feedback on what they did well and areas they can work on. Instead of saying, "You need to hit better," try, "I noticed your swing is improving; let's keep working on it." Celebrate their effort and improvement, regardless of the game's outcome. Praise their dedication, their hustle on the field, and their teamwork. This positive reinforcement helps them see the value in their hard work and keeps them motivated.

Recognizing signs of burnout and stress is crucial. Changes in behavior or attitude, such as becoming more withdrawn or irritable, can be red flags. If your child shows a decreased interest in activities they once enjoyed, it might be a sign they're feeling overwhelmed. Physical symptoms like headaches, stomachaches, and trouble sleeping are stress indicators. Pay close attention to these signs and address them promptly. Open a dialogue with your child, and let them know it's okay to feel this way. Encourage them to take breaks and engage in activities that help them relax and recharge.

Maintaining a healthy balance between sports and other aspects of life is vital. Encourage your child to pursue hobbies and interests outside of baseball. Whether playing an instrument, drawing, or simply spending time with friends, these activities provide a well-rounded experience and prevent burnout. Prioritizing family time and social activities also helps create a balanced life. Family dinners, movie nights, and weekend outings can provide a much-needed break from the routine and strengthen family bonds.

One of my players was incredibly talented but started showing signs of burnout halfway through the season. His parents noticed he was becoming more irritable and less enthusiastic about practice. We had a meeting where we discussed the importance of balance. His parents encouraged him to have an interest in other things beyond baseball. They also made sure to have Conversations where baseball wasn't the focus of discussion. Over time, his attitude improved, and he regained his love for the game.

Balancing encouragement without adding pressure takes mindful effort but pays off in the long run. It's about understanding your child's needs, recognizing the signs of stress, and maintaining a healthy balance between sports and other life aspects. By setting realistic expectations, offering constructive feedback, and celebrating effort, you can help your child thrive on and off the field. Remember, the goal is to nurture their love for the game and support their well-being.

Open Communication with Coaches

Building a solid relationship with your child's coach can make a difference in their development. When parents and coaches agree, a cohesive support system benefits the player. One of the most significant advantages is the alignment of goals and expectations. You can reinforce those principles at home when you understand the coach's objectives and methods. This consistency helps your child navigate their path more smoothly, knowing everyone is working towards the same end.

Understanding your child's needs and progress is another crucial aspect. Regular communication with the coach lets you get a clearer picture of your child's development. How are they performing in practice? What areas need improvement? Are there any behavioral or emotional concerns? This insight can help you provide better support at home, whether by offering extra practice sessions or simply lending a sympathetic ear.

Effective communication strategies are vital to maintaining this open dialogue. Scheduling regular check-ins with the coach can keep you updated on your child's progress and any changes in the training routine. These meetings don't have to be formal; a quick chat after practice can be just as effective. Asking specific questions about your child's development can provide valuable insights. Instead of general queries like "How are they doing?" ask, "How is their swing improving?" or "Do they need to work on their fielding skills?". This shows that you're genuinely interested and engaged.

Being open to feedback and suggestions is essential. Coaches have a wealth of experience and can offer valuable advice. Sometimes, this feedback might be hard to hear, especially if it involves areas where your child needs improvement. However, accepting constructive criticism with an open mind can lead to significant growth. Remember, the coach wants the best for your child, just like you do.

Supporting the coach's role at home can reinforce the lessons learned on the field. Consistency in messaging and expectations helps your child understand that the principles they learn during practice also apply outside of it. *Encourage respect for the coach's authority by backing their decisions and strategies.* When your child sees that you and the coach are united, it reinforces the importance of following their guidance.

It's crucial to handle conflicts and disagreements constructively. Disagreements are natural, but how you address them can make a big difference. Approach conflicts calmly and respectfully. Avoid confrontational language and focus on finding a solution that benefits your child. Seeking compromise and understanding can often resolve issues without escalating tensions. Always keep your child's best interests at heart. It's easy to get caught up in the moment's emotions, but remember that the primary goal is to support your child's development and enjoyment of the sport.

I recall a situation with one of my players whose parents were initially skeptical of my coaching methods. They felt their son wasn't getting enough playing time and were concerned it might affect his confidence. We discussed their concerns. I explained my strategy and how I focused on developing his skills for the long term. They listened, asked specific questions, and we found common ground. They encouraged him to follow my practice routines, and his performance improved. This collaborative approach helped their son thrive both on and off the field.

I will sit down with parents and offer them a blueprint or a roadmap based on what I see so that if they want to help, they can put resources towards what I see would help their son improve. This is an ongoing and evolving process.

Building a solid parent-coach relationship is more than just attending games and cheering from the sidelines. It's about aligning goals, understanding your child's needs, and maintaining open, respectful dialogue. By supporting the coach's role and handling conflicts constructively, you create a cohesive support system that can significantly enhance your child's athletic experience.

Balancing Support and Independence

One of the most rewarding aspects of coaching is watching young athletes grow in skill, confidence, and self-reliance. Fostering independence in children is crucial because it builds a foundation for self-reliance and confidence. When kids learn to take responsibility for their actions, they gain a sense of ownership over their successes and failures. This sense of ownership is vital for developing resilience and preparing for future challenges. Encouraging autonomy helps them navigate the ups and downs of sports and life with a stronger sense of self.

Allowing children to set goals is a powerful way to support their independence. When kids are involved in setting their objectives, they feel more invested in achieving them. Encourage them to think about what they want to accomplish, whether improving their batting average or mastering a new skill. This boosts their motivation and teaches them the importance of goal-setting and planning. Problem-solving and decision-making are other critical skills. When your child faces a challenge, resist the urge to step in immediately. Instead, guide them through the process of figuring out a solution. Ask questions that prompt them to think critically, such as, "What do you think you could do differently next time?" This approach helps them develop problem-solving skills and confidence in handling difficult situations.

Supporting self-reflection and self-assessment is another way to encourage independence. After a game or practice, ask your child to reflect on their performance. What did they do well? What could they improve? This practice helps them become more self-aware and take responsibility for their growth. It also fosters a mindset of continuous improvement, which is essential for success in any endeavor.

Finding the right balance between involvement and independence can be challenging. Knowing when to step back and let your child lead is essential. This doesn't mean abandoning them to figure everything out on their own. Instead, guide without taking control. Offer support and advice, but let them make their own decisions and learn from their experiences. This approach builds their confidence and teaches them valuable life skills.

My degree in education and psychology helped create balance in my player's lives. One family I worked with found an outstanding balance between support and independence. Their son was talented but struggled with decision-making on the field. His parents decided to let him take the lead in setting his goals and figuring out how to achieve them. They provided support by discussing his goals and offering advice, but they let him make the final decisions. Over time, he became more confident in his abilities and took more initiative on and off the field. His parents noticed a significant improvement in his performance and overall demeanor.

Balancing support and independence is about more than just stepping back. It's about creating an environment where your child feels empowered to take risks, make mistakes, and learn from them. It's about providing the proper guidance and support without overshadowing their efforts. Doing so, you help them develop the self-reliance and confidence they need to navigate the challenges they'll face in sports and beyond.

Supporting independence in your child is a continuous process that involves allowing them to set their own goals, encouraging problem-solving and decision-making, and fostering self-reflection and self-assessment. It's about finding the balance between being supportive and giving them the space to grow. Doing so, you help them build the self-reliance and confidence needed to face future challenges head-on.

Fostering Resilience in Everyday Life

Resilience is the ability to recover from setbacks and adapt to challenges. In a young athlete's life, resilience means bouncing back after a tough loss, a missed play, or even an injury. It's about having the emotional strength to keep going, no matter what obstacles come their way. Resilience is crucial because it helps children handle the ups and downs of sports and life. It teaches them that failure is not the end but a stepping stone to success. Emotional adaptability is another crucial aspect. It allows children to adjust their mindset and approach when faced with new or difficult situations, helping them stay focused and motivated.

Building resilience at home starts with encouraging a growth mindset. A growth mindset is the belief that abilities and intelligence can be developed through dedication and hard work. Encourage your child to see challenges as growth opportunities rather than insurmountable obstacles. Praise their effort and persistence, not just their achievements. This helps them understand that success results from hard work and learning from mistakes. Teaching problem-solving skills is another essential technique. When your child faces a problem, guide them through finding a solution. Ask questions like, "What do you think you could try next?" or "How might you approach this differently?" This empowers them to tackle challenges independently and builds their confidence.

Modeling resilient behavior is equally important. Children learn a lot by observing their parents. Show them how you handle setbacks in your own life. Talk about times when things didn't go as planned and how you overcame those challenges. Demonstrate a positive attitude and a willingness to keep trying, even when things get tough. This sets a powerful example for your child and shows them that resilience is a valuable trait.

Incorporating resilience-building activities into your daily routine can also make a big difference. Role-playing challenging scenarios is a fun and practical way to teach resilience. For example, you can simulate a challenging game situation and ask your child how they would handle it. This helps them practice problem-solving and decision-making in a safe environment. Discussing stories of overcoming adversity can be inspiring. Share examples of athletes or other figures who faced significant challenges and came out stronger on the other side. This can motivate your child and show them that resilience leads to success.

Practicing gratitude and positive thinking is another effective method. Encourage your child to keep a gratitude journal where they write down things they are thankful for daily. This helps them focus on the positive aspects of their life and develop a more optimistic outlook. Positive thinking can also be fostered through affirmations and self-talk. Teach your child to replace negative thoughts with positive ones. For instance, instead of thinking, "I'll never get this right," encourage them to say, "I can improve with practice." This shift in mindset can significantly boost their resilience.

I've seen firsthand how these techniques can foster resilience in young athletes. We don't get involved with role-playing, but we do teach resilience. Baseball is probably the most demanding sport you can play because there are a lot of failures, so we teach resilience by explaining to the players that they need to have a short memory on the field to move on to the next play and realize that there is always an opportunity to do some good on the next play. Even if my players are having a rough day or had a poor outing in the previous game, we teach them that no one is perfect, to let it go and refocus on doing the best job on the next play.

Fostering resilience in children is about more than just helping them succeed in sports. It's about preparing them for the challenges they'll face in life. By encouraging a growth mindset, teaching problem-solving skills, modeling resilient behavior, and incorporating resilience-building activities, you can help your child develop the emotional strength and adaptability they need to thrive.

As we wrap up this chapter, remember that parental involvement plays a crucial role in a child's development. From creating a positive home environment to balancing support and independence, your actions and attitudes significantly impact your growth. In the next chapter, we'll explore advanced mental strategies for high school athletes, diving into techniques to help them excel at the next level.

6

ADVANCED MENTAL STRATEGIES FOR HIGH SCHOOL ATHLETES

I vividly recall a particular high school game that perfectly encapsulated the importance of mental strategies. We were up against our cross town, rival, and we were under duress. Our best picture had been having an incredible season, but that day, he seemed off. He was visibly shaken when he walked two batters in a row during a crucial inning. I called for a time out and walked to the mound. I told him "we have every confidence in the world you can execute and get us off the field." I also told him what I believe will happen if he execute a pitch, breathes, and then repeats.

This kind of scenario demonstrated the power of advanced visualization techniques in high-pressure situations.

Advanced Visualization Techniques

Visualization, or mental imagery or rehearsal, is a cognitive technique in which you create vivid mental images and scenarios. It's not just about picturing isolated actions but entire game scenarios. Imagine walking onto the field, the noise of the crowd, the feel of your glove, and the smell of the fresh-cut grass. Visualizing these full scenes activates the same neural pathways in your brain as actual physical execution, strengthening those neural connections and priming your body for optimal performance.

Using all five senses in visualization enhances its effectiveness. For example, don't just see the ball moving from glove to glove when visualizing a fast double play. Feel the glove's leather on your hand, hear the satisfying pop as the ball hits the pocket, and smell the fresh-cut grass. This multi-sensory approach makes the experience more realistic and impactful. Practicing visualization under various conditions, such as imagining playing in different weather or with distracting crowd noise, can prepare you for any situation. Picture yourself making a critical play in the rain or staying focused despite heckling fans. This practice can help you remain composed and perform well despite external conditions.

Visualization techniques can be tailored to specific roles in the field. Infielders can benefit from visualizing fast double plays. Picture yourself fielding the ball cleanly, pivoting smoothly, and making a quick, accurate throw to first base. This mental practice can improve your reaction time and precision during actual games. Pitchers can visualize different pitch sequences. Imagine the grip of the ball, the windup, and the release. Visualize striking out a batter with a perfect curveball or fastball. This can help you stay focused and confident on the mound. Batters can visualize various pitch types and their responses. Picture the trajectory of a curveball, a fastball, or a slider, and see yourself making solid contact. This mental preparation can improve your pitch recognition and hitting accuracy.

Combining visualization with physical practice can maximize its effectiveness. Before executing plays in practice, take a moment to visualize the play. See yourself making the perfect catch, throw, or hit. This mental rehearsal can enhance your muscle memory and coordination. Using visualization during warm-ups can also be beneficial. Spend a few minutes before each game visualizing key plays and scenarios. This can set a positive tone and boost your confidence. By integrating mental and physical training, you can create a comprehensive preparation routine that covers all aspects of your performance.

Tracking the impact of visualization is crucial to understanding its effectiveness. Keeping a visualization journal can help. After each visualization session, jot down what you visualized and how it felt. Note any improvements in your performance linked to visualization. Over time, this can help you identify patterns and refine your visualization techniques. Assessing performance improvements related to visualization can provide valuable insights. Compare your performance before and after incorporating visualization into your routine. Look for improvements in focus, confidence, and execution. This self-assessment can help you understand the value of visualization and motivate you to continue practicing it.

Every day, the first thing we do in practice is to have our kids lie down on the grass and be still for two minutes. They are told to forget everything that's happened before practice and then try to visualize some success on the field. It's stepping into the batter's box and hitting, executing a pitch, or fielding a ground ball. That's sort of how we do visualization. The power of advanced visualization techniques boosted fuck off performance and confidence.

Visualization is not just a mental exercise; it's a powerful tool that can transform your game. You can unlock new performance and mental readiness levels by diving deep into advanced visualization techniques, tailoring them to specific roles, combining them with physical practice, and tracking their impact. Visualization can help you stay focused, confident, and prepared for any situation on the field, whether you're an infielder, pitcher, or batter. Handling the

Pressure of Recruiting

The recruiting process for high school baseball players can be a mix of excitement and pressure, with college recruiters evaluating your skills on the field and looking at how you handle adversity. While it's essential to focus on your mechanics and athleticism, recruiters are equally interested in your mental toughness, character, and team player ability. They're watching how you perform under pressure and how quickly you bounce back from mistakes. You must be physically and mentally ready to stand out by showing resilience and a positive attitude, even when things don't go perfectly.

That pressure to perform can feel overwhelming, especially when you know every move is being scrutinized. Whether you pitch or hit, it's easy to overthink every action, worrying that one mistake could ruin your chances. The key is to develop techniques to stay calm and focused, such as breathing exercises or visualizing success. Instead of trying to impress the recruiters, concentrate on doing your best and enjoying the game. This mental shift can ease the stress, allowing you to play more naturally and confidently.

Balancing personal performance with team success is another challenge. While you want to shine in front of scouts, you're also part of a team, and finding that balance between individual achievement and contributing to team victories is essential. At the same time, external pressures from parents, coaches, and friends can add to the stress, especially when you feel like you're playing for their approval. This is why maintaining a positive mindset is crucial. Embrace feedback as a chance to grow, not as criticism, and focus on improving yourself. Remember, recruiters are looking for coachable players with a strong work ethic. By preparing both physically and mentally, you can manage the pressures of the recruiting process and present yourself as a well-rounded player ready for the next level.

Mental Preparation for Big Games

Regarding high-stakes games, mental preparation is as crucial as physical training. Imagine stepping onto the field for a championship game with all eyes on you. The pressure can be immense; this is where mental readiness makes a difference. Being mentally prepared not only impacts your performance but also boosts your confidence. It helps you handle game-day nerves, stay focused, and perform best when it matters most. Mental preparation can differ between a clutch performance and a missed opportunity.

Creating a pre-game mental checklist can help you get into the right mindset before a big game. Start by setting specific mental goals for the game. What do you want to achieve mentally? Maybe it's staying calm under pressure or maintaining focus throughout the game. Write these goals down and review them before you step onto the field. Visualization of game scenarios and responses is another critical element. Spend a few minutes visualizing different game situations and how you will respond. Picture yourself making the perfect play, hitting the ball solidly, or striking out a batter. This mental rehearsal can make you feel more prepared and confident. Incorporate relaxation techniques to help reduce pre-game anxiety. Techniques like deep breathing, progressive muscle relaxation, or listening to calming music can help you stay relaxed and focused.

On game day, several techniques can ensure you're mentally ready. Mindfulness exercises can help you stay present. Take a few moments to focus on your breath and clear your mind of distractions. This can help you stay grounded and focused on the task at hand. Positive self-talk and affirmations are also powerful tools. Remind yourself of your strengths and abilities. Repeat positive statements like, "I am ready" or "I can handle this." These affirmations can boost your confidence and help you maintain a positive mindset. Focus drills can help you maintain concentration. For example, practice focusing on a specific point, like the catcher's mitt or the ball, to help keep your mind sharp and avoid distractions.

Athletes who excel in big games often attribute their success to mental preparation. Consider the case of David Ortiz in the 2004 ALCS. Ortiz's mental readiness was evident as he made clutch hits in high-pressure situations, helping the Red Sox make a historic comeback. His ability to stay calm and focused under immense pressure resulted from rigorous mental preparation. Another example is Serena Williams, who uses visualization and positive self-talk to prepare for big matches. Her mental toughness and preparation have contributed to her numerous Grand Slam titles.

In my coaching career, I've seen firsthand the impact of mental preparation on performance. One player struggled with nerves before big games. We developed a pre-game mental checklist that included specific mental goals, visualization of game scenarios, and relaxation techniques. On game day, he practiced positive self-talk. Over time, his confidence grew, and his performance in high-stakes games improved. He went from being overwhelmed by pressure to thriving in it, demonstrating the power of mental preparation.

The importance of mental preparation for key games cannot be overstated. It impacts your performance and confidence, helping you handle game-day nerves and perform at your best. By creating a personalized pre-game mental checklist, practicing mindfulness, using positive self-talk, and incorporating focus drills, you can ensure you're mentally ready for any high-stakes game. The stories of athletes like David Ortiz, Serena Williams, Liam, and Maria highlight the transformative power of mental readiness in achieving clutch performances.

Developing Leadership on the Team

In baseball, leadership isn't just about being the best player on the field but inspiring and guiding your teammates. Influential team leaders possess several key traits that set them apart. First and foremost are communication skills. A strong leader can convey their thoughts clearly and listen to others. They can articulate strategies, provide constructive feedback, and motivate their teammates. Emotional intelligence is another crucial quality. This means being aware of your own emotions and understanding the feelings of others. A leader with high emotional intelligence can navigate the ups and downs of the game, offering support and encouragement when needed. Leading by example is the most visible trait of a good leader. When you work hard, stay positive, and show dedication, your teammates are likelier to follow your lead. They see your commitment and are inspired to match it.

To develop leadership skills, players can take several actionable steps. One effective method is role-playing leadership scenarios. During practice, you can simulate game situations where you must make quick decisions, communicate effectively, and rally your team. This helps you practice leadership in a controlled environment, preparing you for real-game situations. Another valuable technique is participating in mentorship programs with senior players or coaches. A mentor provides guidance, advice, and a model for effective leadership. Learning from someone with more experience can accelerate your growth as a leader. Engage with your mentor, ask questions, and observe how they handle different situations. This hands-on learning is invaluable.

Balancing leadership with personal performance can be challenging. As a leader, you are responsible for guiding your team while maintaining your level of play. Time management strategies are essential. Plan your schedule to ensure time for personal practice and team activities. Prioritize tasks and delegate when necessary. Encouraging team cohesion and trust is also vital. Foster a team environment where everyone feels valued and heard. This strengthens the team and makes your leadership role more manageable. When your teammates trust you and each other, the team functions more smoothly, allowing you to focus on your performance.

Examples of great team leaders can provide inspiration and guidance. Derek Jeter, the former captain of the New York Yankees, is a prime example. Known for his work ethic, composure, and ability to perform under pressure, Jeter was a leader both on and off the field. His teammates respected him for his dedication and ability to stay calm in high-stress situations. Another example is Jackie Robinson, who broke baseball's color barrier. Robinson's courage, resilience, and exceptional talent made him a natural leader. He faced immense pressure and adversity but remained steadfast, inspiring his teammates and paving the way for future generations. These players exemplify the traits of influential leaders—communication, emotional intelligence, and leading by example.

My coaching career has seen many young players develop into outstanding leaders. One such player was not the most talented on the team, but his leadership qualities set him apart. He communicated effectively with his teammates, offering encouragement and constructive feedback. He had high emotional intelligence, always knowing when a teammate needed a boost or advice. Most importantly, he led by example. He was always the first to arrive at practice and the last to leave, setting a standard for the rest of the team. His leadership was instrumental in our team's success that season.

Effective leadership in baseball involves a combination of communication skills, emotional intelligence, and leading by example. Developing these skills through role-playing scenarios and mentorship programs can significantly enhance your leadership abilities. Balancing leadership with personal performance requires time management strategies and fostering team cohesion and trust. The examples of players like Derek Jeter, Jackie Robinson, Mike, and Sarah illustrate the impact of strong leadership on a team's success. Embracing these traits and techniques can help you become an effective leader, inspiring and guiding your teammates to achieve great things on and off the field.

Balancing Academics and Athletics

Balancing school and sports is one of the toughest challenges student-athletes face. You're not just juggling practices and games but also dealing with homework, exams, and projects. Time management becomes a crucial skill. It's easy to feel overwhelmed when your days are packed from morning until night. The fatigue from late-night study sessions and early-morning practices can take a toll. Academic pressure adds another layer of stress. Keeping up with grades while striving to excel in the field can seem challenging. But with some practical strategies, you can find a balance that works.

Creating a balanced schedule is the first step. Start by mapping out your week, including class times, practice sessions, game days, and study periods. Use a planner or a scheduling app to keep everything organized. Prioritize tasks with a to-do list. Break down larger tasks into smaller, manageable steps. This makes them less daunting and helps you stay on track. For instance, if you have a big paper due, break it into research, drafting, and editing phases. Checking off tasks as you complete them can give you a sense of accomplishment and motivate you. Time-blocking is another helpful technique. Allocate specific time slots for studying, practicing, and resting. Stick to your schedule as much as possible to maintain a healthy balance.

Support systems play a significant role in helping student-athletes manage their responsibilities. Don't hesitate to communicate with your teachers about your sports commitments. Let them know when you have games or practices that might conflict with classwork. Most teachers appreciate the heads-up and will work with you on deadlines. Utilize school resources like tutoring and counseling. Many schools offer academic support specifically for student-athletes. Take advantage of these services to stay on top of your studies. Your coaches can also be a valuable resource. They understand the demands of balancing academics and sports and can offer advice and flexibility when needed. Family support is equally important. Tell your family about your schedule and any challenges you face. Their encouragement can provide a much-needed boost.

Let's look at one example of an athlete who excelled academically and in sports. This high school senior, who was a star player and maintained a high GPA, credits his success to strict time management and a supportive network. He used a planner religiously, blocking out time for studying and practicing. He also communicated regularly with his teachers, ensuring he stayed on his assignments. His efforts paid off, and he earned both academic and athletic scholarships.

These stories highlight that it's possible to excel in academics and athletics with the right strategies and support. These responsibilities require discipline, effective time management, and a robust support system. You can manage the demands of being a student-athlete by creating a balanced schedule, prioritizing tasks, and seeking support from teachers, coaches, and family. The lessons learned in balancing school and sports can also prepare you for future challenges, teaching you valuable skills like time management, discipline, and resilience.

As we continue to explore strategies for success in baseball and beyond, the next chapter will delve into the importance of holistic development. We'll discuss how mental and physical health, nutrition, and rest all play a vital role in your overall performance and well-being. Balancing these elements can help you achieve peak performance and lead a fulfilling life on and off the field.

7
COLLEGE-LEVEL MENTAL STRATEGIES

W e teach players to be mentally flexible, to expect the unexpected, and to adapt. The power of mental flexibility in action is impressive.

Examples of mental flexibility in action are abundant in sports. Consider the story of a college baseball player who faced a challenging situation during a crucial game. The opposing team had studied his hitting tendencies and adjusted their pitches accordingly. Instead of sticking to his usual approach, this player adapted his setup, thought process and mechanics, thereby achieving success. His ability to adjust mid-game, helped him secure a win and showcase his mental flexibility.

Coaches often emphasize the importance of this skill. One coach shared, "mental flexibility separates good players from great ones. It's the ability to stay calm, adapt, and succeed, no matter what the game throws at you."

The Importance of Mental Flexibility
Mental flexibility is the ability to adapt to changing circum-

stances and handle unexpected challenges seamlessly. In sports, and especially in baseball, this skill is crucial. Imagine you're a pitcher, and the batter suddenly changes their stance. Or you're a batter, and the pitcher starts throwing curveballs when you were expecting fastballs. Your ability to adjust in these moments can make or break your performance. *Mental flexibility isn't just about reacting to changes; it's about anticipating them and being prepared to pivot when necessary.*

Developing mental flexibility requires practice and intentional strategies. One effective method is cognitive flexibility exercises, which train your brain to switch tasks quickly and efficiently. For instance, you can practice by switching between different drills rapidly during practice sessions. This trains your mind to adapt to new tasks without losing focus. Another practical approach is embracing uncertainty through scenario planning. Spend time visualizing various game scenarios, including the unlikely ones. Consider how you would respond if the opposing team changes their strategy mid-game or if you are in an unexpected situation. This mental rehearsal prepares you to handle surprises with confidence and poise.

Mental flexibility has immense benefits for athletes. First, it enhances problem-solving skills. When you're mentally flexible, you're better equipped to think on your feet and create creative solutions to unexpected challenges. This ability is invaluable during games, where quick thinking can lead to game-changing plays. Mental flexibility also improves decision-making under pressure. Training your mind to adapt quickly allows you to make better decisions in high-stress situations, resulting in more consistent and effective performance.

Additionally, mental flexibility increases resilience. Athletes who can adapt to changing circumstances are more likely to avoid being thrown off by setbacks. They can bounce back quickly and stay focused on their goals, even when things are unplanned.

Examples of mental flexibility in action are abundant in sports. Consider the story of a college baseball player who faced a challenging situation during a crucial game. The opposing team had studied his batting patterns and adjusted their pitches accordingly. Instead of sticking to his usual approach, this player adapted his stance and timing, successfully hitting the new pitches. His ability to adjust mid-game helped his team secure a win and showcased his mental flexibility. Coaches often emphasize the importance of this skill. One coach shared, "Mental flexibility separates good players from great ones. It's the ability to stay calm, adapt, and succeed, no matter what the game throws at you."

Mental Flexibility Exercise

1. Switching Tasks Drill: During practice, set up a series of different drills that require varying skills. Move quickly from one drill to the next, forcing your mind to adjust rapidly. For example, switch from batting practice to fielding ground balls and pitching drills. This exercise trains your brain to adapt quickly to new tasks.
2. Scenario Planning: Spend a few minutes each day visualizing different game scenarios. Think about unexpected situations you might encounter and how you would respond. For example, imagine the opposing team changing their strategy mid-game. Visualize yourself adapting to their new approach and making successful plays. This mental rehearsal prepares you to handle surprises with confidence.

These exercises are simple yet powerful ways to enhance your mental flexibility. Incorporating them into your training routine allows you to develop the adaptability needed to excel in college baseball. Remember, cognitive flexibility isn't just a skill; it's a mindset. Embrace change, expect the unexpected, and stay ready to adapt.

. . .

Peak Performance Techniques

Peak performance is that magical state where everything seems to click. You're not just playing the game; you're dominating it. For college athletes, achieving peak performance means consistently reaching the highest level of their abilities. It's not just about having a great game once in a while; it's about maintaining a high standard of play over an extended period. This consistency is what separates good athletes from great ones. When you're at your peak, you're in the zone—fully immersed, entirely focused, and executing with precision.

One of the most effective ways to reach peak performance is through techniques that induce a flow state. The flow state, often described as"in the zone," is a mental state where you are fully engaged and performing at your best. You can practice flow state induction techniques like setting clear, achievable goals for each practice and game to get into this state. Break your tasks into manageable chunks and focus on one thing at a time. Another method is using visualization combined with physical rehearsal. Before each game, spend a few minutes visualizing yourself executing key plays flawlessly. Then, during practice, physically rehearse these visualized scenarios. This combination helps reinforce muscle memory and boosts confidence.

Pre-competition routines are also crucial for achieving peak performance. Develop a set of rituals that you follow before every game. This could include specific warm-up exercises, mental drills, or even listening to a playlist that gets you pumped. These routines help create a sense of familiarity and control, reducing pre-game anxiety and setting the stage for optimal performance. They also signal to your brain that it's time to focus and perform, making it easier to get into the zone.

Monitoring and sustaining peak performance requires ongoing effort. Regular performance reviews are essential. After each game, take some time to reflect on your performance. Identify what went well and what could be improved. This self-assessment helps you stay aware of your strengths and areas for growth. Adjusting your training based on feedback is another critical aspect. Listen to your coaches, teammates, and even your own body. If something isn't working, be willing to make changes. This adaptability ensures you continue performing at your best without burning out.

By getting into the zone, visualizing, and physically rehearsing these routines into your training, you can elevate your game to new heights. Regular performance reviews and the willingness to adapt will help you sustain this high level of play, ensuring you remain a top performer throughout your college career. These techniques are not just about reaching your peak; they're about staying there and improving.

Stress Management for College Athletes

High school and college athletes face unique stressors that can significantly impact their performance on and off the field. Academic pressures are a huge part of this. Balancing coursework, exams, and projects with daily practices and games can be overwhelming. The constant need to maintain good grades to stay eligible for the team adds another layer of stress. Then there are the athletic commitments. The demands of training, traveling for games, and the pressure to perform at a high level can lead to physical and mental exhaustion. Social expectations can also weigh heavily. College athletes often need to maintain a social life, meet family expectations, and navigate relationships, all while trying to excel in their sports and academics.

Effective stress management is crucial for college athletes to maintain their well-being and performance. One practical strategy is mastering time management and organizational skills. Using planners, digital calendars, or time-blocking techniques can help athletes keep track of their schedules and prioritize tasks. Breaking large assignments into smaller, manageable tasks can make academic work less daunting. Another effective method is practicing mindful ness and relaxation exercises. Techniques such as deep breathing, progressive muscle relaxation, and meditation can help reduce stress and improve focus. These exercises can be incorporated into daily routines, even for just a few minutes each day.

Seeking support from mental health professionals is another valuable strategy. Many colleges offer counseling services for athletes, providing a safe space to discuss stressors and develop coping mechanisms. Mental health professionals can provide personalized strategies to manage stress, anxiety, and other mental health concerns. It's important to remember that seeking help is a sign of strength, not weakness. Professional guidance can make a significant difference in an athlete's ability to handle the pressures of college life.

Balancing multiple responsibilities requires careful planning and a proactive approach. Prioritizing tasks is critical. Athletes must identify their most important daily tasks and focus on completing them first. Setting boundaries is equally important. This might mean saying no to certain social activities or delegating tasks when possible. Using downtime effectively can also help. Instead of wasting free time on unproductive activities, athletes can use these moments for relaxation, mindfulness exercises, or catching up on reading. Small breaks throughout the day can recharge the mind and body, making it easier to handle the demands of college life.

Several athletic departments have implemented stress reduction programs to support their athletes. These programs often include workshops on time management, mindfulness, and self-care practices. They also provide access to mental health professionals and peer support groups. For instance, one college's athletic department introduced a stress management program that included weekly mindfulness sessions, one-on-one counseling, and group workshops on time management and relaxation techniques. Athletes who participated in the program reported feeling less stressed and more focused on their sports and academics.

By employing effective stress management strategies, college athletes can better navigate challenges and maintain their well-being and performance. Mastering time management, practicing mindfulness, or seeking professional support can significantly improve an athlete's ability to handle the pressures of college life.

Long-Term Goal Setting

Long-term goals are the cornerstone of any athlete's career. For college athletes, setting these goals is crucial for guiding their careers and personal development. Imagine stepping onto the field with a clear vision of where you want to be in five or ten years. This vision keeps you motivated, focused, and driven. It's not just about the next game or season; it's about building a foundation for future success. Long-term goals provide a roadmap, giving you direction and purpose, which is particularly important during challenging times when motivation might wane.

Creating practical long-term goals starts with defining clear, achievable milestones. Break down your ultimate goal into smaller, manageable steps. For instance, if your long-term goal is to make it to the professional leagues, identify the skills you need to develop, the statistics you need to hit, and the accolades you need to earn. Each milestone should be specific and measurable, allowing you to track your progress. Next, create a roadmap for achieving these milestones. This roadmap should outline the steps you need to take, the resources you'll need, and the timeline for each phase. Regularly review and adjust your goals as needed. Life is unpredictable, and flexibility is critical. If you encounter setbacks or find that your goals need tweaking, don't hesitate to make adjustments. The important thing is to stay committed and keep moving forward.

Balancing short-term and long-term goals is essential for maintaining motivation and focus. Short-term goals act as stepping stones toward your larger aspirations. They provide immediate targets to aim for, keeping you engaged and motivated. For example, a short-term goal might be to improve your batting average over the next month. This goal aligns with your long-term aspiration of becoming a more consistent hitter. Integrate your short-term performance goals with your long-term career plans. This alignment ensures that every practice, every game, and every effort contributes to your overall objective. Stay adaptable and open to change. Your goals evolve as you grow and gain more experience. Embrace this evolution and be willing to adjust your plans accordingly.

Athletes who set long-term goals often find more tremendous success and fulfillment. These goals provide direction, keep you motivated, and help you navigate the ups and downs of your athletic career. By defining clear milestones, creating a roadmap, balancing short-term and long-term objectives, and staying adaptable, you can achieve your aspirations and build a rewarding career in sports. The stories of athletes like Alex and Emily highlight the transformative power of goal setting, offering valuable lessons for anyone looking to achieve their dreams in college athletics and beyond.

Using Mental Breaks Effectively

Mental breaks are short periods where you step away from intense focus or physical exertion to relax and recharge. These breaks are crucial for athletes because they prevent burnout and enhance focus and productivity. Imagine running a marathon without water stations—eventually, your performance would plummet. Mental breaks serve as those essential water stations, helping you maintain peak performance over the long haul. They allow your brain to reset, reducing the mental fatigue that can build up from continuous effort.

One effective technique for incorporating mental breaks into your routine is scheduling regular downtime and relaxation periods. This can be as simple as taking a 10-minute break every hour to stretch, breathe deeply, or sit quietly. Another strategy is engaging in non-sport activities you enjoy, like hobbies or socializing with friends. These activities provide a mental shift that helps your brain relax and recover. For instance, you might find that playing a musical instrument, reading a book, or spending time with loved ones enables you to unwind and recharge.

The benefits of regular mental breaks are significant. First, they improve mental clarity. When you give your brain a chance to rest, you return to your tasks with a clearer mind and better focus. This can lead to more efficient and effective practice sessions. Mental breaks also reduce stress and anxiety, which are common in high-pressure environments like college sports. By taking time to relax, you lower your stress levels, making it easier to stay calm and composed during games. Additionally, mental breaks can increase your motivation and energy levels. When you allow yourself to rest, you avoid burnout and maintain a higher enthusiasm for your sport.

The primary thing we do regarding a mental break is take time off. At Thanksgiving, we shut down and took a mental break, and during Christmas week throughout the year, we shut down to take a mental break. After the season ends, the team takes a break for a week.

They can still work out to stay in shape but should avoid any competitive environment.

Several athletic departments have recognized the importance of mental breaks and implemented programs to support their athletes. For instance, one college introduced a "Mental Wellness Week," during which athletes participated in various relaxation and mindfulness activities, such as guided meditation, nature walks, and creative workshops. The program aimed to reduce stress and promote mental well-being, and the feedback from athletes was overwhelmingly positive. Many reported feeling more relaxed, focused, and motivated, highlighting the significant impact of mental breaks on their overall well-being and performance.

Incorporating mental breaks into your routine is not just a luxury; it's a necessity for maintaining peak performance and well-being. By scheduling regular downtime, engaging in enjoyable non-sport activities, and recognizing the benefits of mental breaks, you can prevent burnout, enhance focus, and boost your motivation and energy levels. The experiences of athletes like Rachel and Michael demonstrate the transformative power of mental breaks, offering valuable lessons for anyone looking to maintain a balanced and successful athletic career.

8

EFFECTIVE TEAM COMMUNICATION

I remember a particular season with my high school team where we had immense talent but struggled to play cohesively. We had very good players, but something was missing. The turning point came during a practice session when one of our captains, Mike, opened up about his challenges balancing school, baseball and personal life. His vulnerability created a ripple effect. Other players began sharing their struggles, and a deep sense of trust formed. That season, we went onto compete for a league championship and it wasn't just our skills that got us there.

Another example comes from my college coaching experience. We had developed a unique set of hand and verbal signs to communicate different pitching strategies. This system allowed our pitcher and catcher to communicate without tipping off the opposing team. Overtime, the signals became second nature, and our communication on the field was seamless. The players felt more connected and confident in their roles knowing they had a way to communicate quickly and effectively. This shared language played a crucial role in our success that season, allowing us to execute complex strategies, precisely by developing a team language.

. . .

Building Trust Among Teammates

Trust is the bedrock of any successful team. It binds teammates together, creating the chemistry needed for peak performance. When players trust each other, they will cooperate and collaborate effectively. This trust enhances teamwork, as players feel confident relying on one another. It also increases the willingness to take risks, knowing that their teammates have their backs. In baseball, this might mean a fielder diving for a catch, trusting that the backup will cover if they miss, or a pitcher throwing a challenging pitch, confident in the catcher's ability to handle it.

Building trust among teammates requires intentional strategies. One of the most effective ways is through team-building activities. These activities range from simple icebreaker games to more complex challenges requiring cooperation. For instance, organizing a team outing or participating in a ropes course can help players bond outside the typical baseball environment. These activities build camaraderie and a sense of unity, essential for fostering trust. Another critical strategy is promoting open and honest communication practices. Encourage players to express their thoughts and feelings openly about their performance, team dynamics, or personal challenges. Creating an environment where players feel safe to share without judgment builds a strong foundation of trust. Consistent support and encouragement from both coaches and teammates further reinforce this trust. Recognize and celebrate efforts and achievements, no matter how small they may seem. This consistent positive reinforcement shows players that they are valued and supported.

Vulnerability plays a crucial role in building trust. When players are willing to share their personal stories and challenges, it humanizes them and fosters empathy among teammates. Encouraging players to share their experiences, fears, and aspirations can create deeper connections. This practice strengthens team bonds and builds a supportive environment where players feel understood and valued. For example, players might share their struggle to balance academics and sports during a team meeting. This openness can lead to others offering support, advice, or simply understanding, strengthening the team dynamic.

Several teams have successfully built trust through these strategies. Take the 2004 Boston Red Sox, for example. Known for their "Idiots" moniker, they embraced each other's quirks and vulnerabilities, creating a strong sense of unity and trust. This camaraderie was a driving force behind their historic World Series win. Testimonials from players often highlight the importance of trust in their success. One player shared, "Knowing my teammates had my back allowed me to play confidently and take risks I wouldn't have otherwise." Another player mentioned how team-building activities helped them see their teammates as more than just players, fostering a deeper connection and trust.

Trust-Building Exercise

1. Team Storytelling: Organize a session where each player shares a personal story or challenge. This exercise encourages vulnerability and empathy, fostering more profound connections. Encourage players to listen actively and offer support.
2. Trust Falls is a classic but effective exercise in which players take turns falling backward into the arms of their teammates. This activity builds physical trust and reinforces the idea that teammates are there to catch you when you fall.
3. Team Challenges: Engage in activities that require cooperation, such as building a structure using limited materials or solving a puzzle together. These challenges promote teamwork and collaboration, which are essential for building trust.

By incorporating these exercises into your routine, you can create an environment where trust flourishes, leading to better cooperation, enhanced performance, and a more vital team dynamic. Trust is not built overnight, but with consistent effort, open communication, and a willingness to be vulnerable, your team can develop the confidence needed to succeed.

Conflict Resolution Techniques

Conflict within a baseball team is almost inevitable. Whether it's personality clashes, competition for positions, or simple miscommunication, these issues can disrupt team harmony and performance. I remember a season when two of our star players constantly butted heads. One was intense and driven, while the other was more laid-back but equally talented. Their differing personalities created tension that began affecting the entire team. We had to address the issue head-on to prevent it from derailing our season.

One of the familiar sources of conflict in teams is personality clashes. Players come from various backgrounds, each with unique traits and ways of interacting. When these personalities collide, it can lead to misunderstandings and friction. Another primary source is competition for positions. In baseball, everyone wants to be in the starting lineup, and this healthy competition can sometimes turn sour, leading to resentment and jealousy. Miscommunication is another frequent culprit. A simple misunderstanding can spiral into a significant conflict if not addressed promptly. For example, a missed signal during a game can be interpreted as a lack of trust or respect, escalating team tensions.

Resolving conflicts requires practical and effective techniques. Active listening is one of the most crucial skills in conflict resolution. When players feel heard and understood, they're more likely to open up and work towards a resolution. Encourage players to listen to each other without interrupting and to acknowledge each other's viewpoints. Another effective method is mediation and facilitation.

As a coach, stepping in as a neutral party to facilitate discussions can help resolve disputes. This might involve a meeting where both parties can express their concerns and work towards a solution. Developing a conflict resolution protocol can also be beneficial. Establishing clear guidelines for addressing conflicts ensures everyone knows the steps to take when issues arise, promoting a systematic and fair approach.

Communication plays a pivotal role in preventing and resolving conflicts. Encouraging open dialogue within the team can prevent misunderstandings from escalating. Create an environment where players feel comfortable expressing their concerns and grievances. Setting clear expectations and boundaries is also essential. When everyone understands their roles and expectations, there's more room for communication and conflict. For instance, during team meetings, make it a point to outline each player's responsibilities and the team's overall goals. This clarity helps align everyone's efforts and reduces the chances of conflicts arising from unmet expectations.

I've seen firsthand how effective communication can resolve conflicts and strengthen team unity. One season, we had a situation where two players were constantly at odds over who should be the starting pitcher. Their rivalry was affecting team morale. We held a mediation session where both players could air their grievances. By the end of the session, they better understood each other's perspectives and agreed to support each other, regardless of who started. This open dialogue resolved their conflict and brought the team closer together.

Another example comes from the 2016 Chicago Cubs. During their historic World Series run, the team faced internal conflicts from immense pressure and high expectations. The coaching staff implemented regular team meetings where players could voice their concerns and work through issues collectively. This approach helped resolve conflicts and fostered a supportive environment, ultimately contributing to their success. Testimonials from players often highlight the importance of addressing conflicts head-on. One player shared, "Resolving our differences made us stronger as a team. We learned to communicate better and support each other, which showed in our performance on the field."

Conflict Resolution Exercise

1. Active Listening Drill: Pair up players and have them practice active listening. One player shares a concern while the other listens attentively and summarizes what they heard. This exercise helps players develop empathy and improve their listening skills.
2. Role-Playing Scenarios: Create scenarios that mimic common conflicts, such as disagreements over playing time or strategy. Have players role-play these situations and practice resolving them through open communication and mediation.
3. Conflict Resolution Protocol: Develop a clear protocol for addressing conflicts within the team. Outline players' steps when a dispute arises, such as speaking to a coach or mediating a discussion. This protocol ensures a fair and consistent approach to conflict resolution.

By incorporating these exercises and techniques, you can create a team environment where conflicts are addressed constructively, fostering a more robust, cohesive unit. Conflict, when managed effectively, can lead to growth, innovation, and stronger relationships within the team.

Effective Team Meetings

Our team was struggling mid-season. We had the talent, but something wasn't clicking. I decided to hold a team meeting, not just any meeting, but one designed to get everyone on the same page. The purpose of these team meetings is to facilitate open communication and align team goals and objectives. It's a chance for everyone to voice their thoughts and concerns, creating a more cohesive unit. When players feel heard, they're more likely to buy into the team's vision and work towards common goals. In that meeting, we discussed our strengths and areas for improvement and set clear, achievable goals for the rest of the season. It was a turning point.

Conducting productive meetings involves setting clear agendas and encouraging participation from all team members. Start by outlining what you want to accomplish in the meeting. This could be discussing upcoming games, reviewing past performances, or planning team events. A clear agenda keeps the meeting focused and ensures that all critical topics are covered. Encourage everyone to participate. This could be as simple as asking each player to share their thoughts on a particular subject or having small group discussions before bringing ideas to the larger group. This involvement makes players feel valued and invested in the team's success. Keep the meetings time-efficient. No one wants to sit through a long, drawn-out meeting. Aim for concise, focused discussions that respect everyone's time.

Leadership plays a crucial role in ensuring these meetings are productive. As a coach, you need to lead by example. Show up prepared, stay focused, and model the behavior you expect from your players. Facilitate discussions rather than dominate them. Ask open-ended questions to get players talking and guide the conversation to ensure it stays on track. Summarize key points and action items at the end of the meeting. This helps ensure everyone knows what was discussed and what needs to be done next. It also provides a sense of closure and direction, reinforcing the goals and strategies discussed during the meeting.

I've seen teams transform through effective meetings. Take the case of a college team I worked with. They held regular team meetings where players could voice their opinions and contribute to decision-making. These meetings fostered a sense of ownership and accountability among

the players. One player shared, "Our meetings made me feel like my opin-
ions mattered. It brought us closer as a team and improved our perfor-
mance on the field." Another coach I know emphasized setting clear
agendas and keeping meetings focused. He noted, "When everyone knows
what to expect and what's expected of them, meetings become more
productive and impactful."

Developing a Team Language

Creating a shared team language can significantly enhance
communication and cohesion. A unique team language fosters a
sense of unity and identity, making players feel like they are part of
something special. It also simplifies complex communication during
games, allowing players to convey strategies and signals quickly and
efficiently. Developing specific terms and phrases for plays and
strategy is a great starting point. For example, you might create code
words for different pitches or defensive setups. Using non-verbal
signals, such as hand gestures or body language cues, can also be
incredibly effective, especially in noisy environments where verbal
communication might be challenging.

My teams typically implemented baseball signs to enhance and
execute strategies. The team language is very detailed, and we use it offen-
sively and defensively, as that is how we communicate.

Regularly practicing and reinforcing this language is crucial.
Incorporate it into daily practices and games to become second
nature to the players. The team's culture plays a significant role in
developing this language. Encourage creativity and input from all
team members. This inclusion makes the language more meaningful
and ensures everyone is on the same page. Integrating cultural and
regional influences can also add a unique touch to the team
language, making it more relatable and memorable for the players.

Many successful sports teams have developed their unique
languages. Take the New England Patriots, for example. They have a
highly sophisticated system of codes and signals that allows them to

communicate complex strategies quickly and effectively. Testimonials from players often highlight the sense of unity and identity that a shared language creates. One player mentioned, "Our team language made us feel like we had our secret code. It brought us closer and made communication on the field seamless." Another player shared, "Learning our team language was like being initiated into a special club. It made me feel more connected to my teammates and our goals."

Developing a Team Language

Creating a unique team language is like developing a secret code only your team understands. This shared language can significantly enhance communication and cohesion, making your team feel more united. When everyone on the team knows the specific terms and phrases used during games, it simplifies complex communication. For example, instead of explaining a whole strategy during a game, you can use a single word or phrase that everyone instantly understands. This quick communication can make a huge difference, especially in high-pressure situations where every second counts.

Developing this team language involves a few key steps. First, create specific terms and phrases for standard plays and strategies. These could be code words for different types of pitches, defensive setups, or batting strategies. The key is to make these terms easy to remember and relevant to your team. Next, incorporate non-verbal signals into your team's language. These can be hand signals, gestures, or even eye movements that convey specific messages. Non-verbal signals are instrumental in noisy environments where verbal communication might be challenging. Regularly practice and reinforce this language in your daily routines. Make it a part of your drills and scrimmages so that it becomes second nature to the players. The more you use and reinforce the language, the more ingrained it will become.

The culture of your team plays a significant role in developing this language. Encourage creativity and input from all team members when creating the language. This inclusion makes everyone feel invested in the process and ensures the language is meaningful to the team. Integrate cultural and regional influences to make the language more relatable and memorable. For instance, if your team is from a particular region or has a specific cultural background, incorporate elements of that culture into your team language. This makes the language unique and strengthens the team's identity and unity.

Several teams have successfully developed their unique languages, and their stories highlight the impact of this practice. One notable example is the New York Yankees. They have a highly sophisticated system of codes and signals that allows them to communicate complex strategies quickly and efficiently. This system has been a critical factor in their success over the years. In one instance, during a crucial playoff game, the Yankees used their unique language to execute a perfectly timed double play that turned the game in their favor. The players later credited their ability to communicate seamlessly as a critical factor in their victory.

Testimonials from their players also emphasized the importance of a shared language in building team cohesion. One player shared, "Our team language made us feel like we had our secret code. It brought us closer and made communication on the field seamless." Another player mentioned how learning the team language was like being initiated into a particular club, making them feel more connected to their teammates and the team's goals. These experiences highlight how a shared language can foster a sense of unity and identity, ultimately enhancing team performance.

Another example comes from a college baseball team I coached. We developed a unique set of hand signals to communicate different pitching strategies. This system allowed our pitcher and catcher to communicate without tipping off the opposing team. Over time, these signals became second nature, and our communication on the field was seamless. The players felt more connected and confident in their roles, knowing they had a way to communicate quickly and effectively. This shared language played a crucial role in our success that season, allowing us to execute complex strategies precisely.

By developing a team language, you can create a sense of unity and identity that enhances communication and performance. This language simplifies complex communication, making it easier for players to understand and execute strategies quickly. Encourage creativity and input from all team members and integrate cultural and regional influences to make the language more relatable and memorable. Practice and reinforce the language regularly to become second nature to the players. This shared language can be a powerful tool in building a cohesive and successful team.

The Role of the Coach in Team Dynamics

The coach's role in shaping team dynamics and communication cannot be overstated. As a coach, you set the tone for how the team interacts, both on and off the field. When you emphasize open and respectful communication, you create an environment where players feel comfortable expressing their thoughts and concerns. This openness fosters trust and collaboration, which are crucial for team success. By modeling effective communication behaviors, such as active listening and clear, concise speech, you show your players how to interact respectfully and constructively. Your behavior sets an example that players are likely to follow, influencing the overall communication culture of the team.

One of the most impactful ways to enhance team communication is regular one-on-one check-ins with players. These check-ins provide a private space for players to discuss their concerns, seek advice, and receive constructive feedback. Regular individual conversations help you understand each player's unique challenges and strengths, allowing you to tailor your coaching approach to meet their needs. Additionally, facilitating team-building activities can significantly improve communication. Activities like group challenges or social outings help players bond and learn to communicate more effectively in a relaxed setting. Encouraging feedback and open dialogue during team meetings or practice sessions is also essential. When players know their opinions are valued, they are more likely to engage in meaningful conversations that benefit the team.

Balancing authority and approachability is a delicate but essential aspect of effective coaching. As a coach, you must set clear boundaries and expectations to maintain discipline and ensure the team operates smoothly. However, being approachable is equally essential. Players must feel they can come to you with their concerns without fear of judgment or retribution. Being available and open to listening shows that you care about their well-being and are committed to their growth. This balance creates a supportive environment where players feel respected and motivated to perform their best. For example, you can establish open office hours where players can drop by to discuss issues, fostering a culture of open communication.

Effective coaches understand the importance of these dynamics and implement strategies to enhance team communication. Consider the example of Coach Mike Krzyzewski of Duke University. Known for his excellent communication skills, Coach K has built a basketball dynasty by fostering a culture of trust and open dialogue. He regularly meets with players individually to understand their perspectives and address their concerns. His approachable nature and effective communication have been instrumental in his team's consistent success. Testimonials from his players often highlight how his open-door policy and active listening have made them feel valued and understood, contributing significantly to their performance and team cohesion.

Another example is Coach Pat Summitt, the legendary women's basketball coach at the University of Tennessee. Coach Summitt was known for her tough but caring approach. She set high expectations for her players and made herself available. Her ability to balance authority with approachability earned her immense respect from her players. Many of her players have credited her open communication style for developing on and off the court. One player shared, "Coach Summitt always pushed us to be our best, but she was also there to listen and support us. Her open communication made us stronger as a team."

As a coach, embracing these principles can transform your team dynamics. You can create an environment where players thrive by setting the tone for respectful communication, regularly checking in with players, facilitating team-building activities, and balancing authority with approachability. Effective communication enhances team performance and builds a strong, cohesive unit to tackle any challenge.

This chapter explored how building trust, resolving conflicts, holding effective team meetings, and developing a shared language can enhance team dynamics. As we move forward, we'll delve into advanced gameplay strategies that can further elevate your team's performance.

9
INSPIRATIONAL STORIES AND REAL-LIFE EXAMPLES

Overcoming Adversity: Stories from the Field

One of the most inspiring moments I've had coaching happened during a college game when our outfielder faced an impossible challenge. During a routine practice, he suffered a severe knee injury that doctors said could end his career. He was devastated, but he refused to give up. He threw himself into rehabilitation, using visualization and mental rehearsal to keep his focus and spirits high. Imagining himself running, catching, and hitting helped him stay connected to the game he loved. Every day, he repeated positive affirmations, telling himself, "I am strong; I will come back stronger." His teammates rallied around him, providing a support network that lifted him through the darkest days.

Six months later, he returned to the field as a player and a beacon of resilience. His perseverance paid off when he made a game-saving catch that season, reminding everyone that mental strength can overcome physical limitations. This experience didn't just shape his athletic career; it transformed his personal life, making him more resilient and determined. His story is a testament to the power of mental strategies like visualization, positive self-talk, and community support.

Consider the story of a college pitcher who faced a series of big errors over the course of several games. Each lost weight heavily on him, but he refused to be defeated. He started a journal where he analyzed each game's events, emotions, and reactions. He met regularly with the coaches to discuss his findings and get feedback. With this newfound clarity, he set a specific goals for each practice session, focusing on improving one aspect of his game at a time. His dedication paid off, and by the end of the season, he had not only improved his performance, but also became a team leader, inspiring others with his resilience. In baseball, comebacks are inspiring.

Similarly, in Major League Baseball, stories of overcoming adversity are plentiful. Josh Hamilton's tale is one of the most notable. Hamilton faced severe addiction issues that derailed his early career. After years of struggle, he found his way back through relentless mental and emotional work. Visualization played a crucial role in his recovery, helping him focus on his goals and imagine a future free from addiction. Positive self-talk and affirmations helped him rebuild his confidence. His support network, including former teammates and mentors, encouraged him to stay on track. Hamilton's comeback was miraculous, culminating in winning the American League MVP 2010. His journey from the depths of addiction to the pinnacle of baseball is a powerful example of how mental resilience can change the course of a life.

Another story that resonates deeply is that of Jon Lester, who was diagnosed with non-Hodgkin's lymphoma in 2006. Facing cancer is daunting for anyone, let alone an athlete at the peak of his career. Lester used mental imagery to picture himself healthy and back on the mound, motivating him through grueling treatments. He also leaned heavily on positive self-talk, constantly reminding himself that he was more than his diagnosis. The Boston Red Sox community, including his teammates and fans, became his support system, cheering him on in and out of the hospital. Lester's successful battle against cancer and subsequent return to baseball, where he helped the Red Sox win the World Series in 2007, is a testament to the unyielding power of mental toughness and community support.

Jim Morris's story is another remarkable example. A high school teacher who had given up baseball due to injuries, Morris made an improbable comeback at 35, inspired by a bet with his students. His visualization and mental rehearsal during his journey back to the mound were pivotal. He visualized every pitch and every game scenario and used positive self-talk to maintain his belief that he could make it. His students and family formed a robust support network, encouraging him every step of the way. Morris's debut in the Major Leagues and subsequent success proved that it's never too late to chase your dreams, no matter how unlikely they seem.

Jackie Robinson's story is one of the most significant in the history of baseball. Breaking the color barrier in 1947, Robinson faced unimaginable racism and hostility. His mental strategies were his armor. He relied on visualization to see himself succeeding despite the odds, and his positive self-talk kept him motivated in the face of relentless adversity. Robinson built a network of supporters, including Dodgers' executive Branch Rickey and his teammates, who stood by him. His resilience shaped his Hall of Fame career and paved the way for future generations of athletes, demonstrating how mental strength can break down barriers and change the world.

These stories underline how mental strategies like visualization, positive self-talk, and building a support network can help athletes overcome significant challenges. Whether it's recovering from a career-threatening injury, facing severe game slumps, or dealing with personal tragedies, these mental tools are crucial. They help overcome adversity and build increased resilience, enhance leadership qualities, and shape one's career and personal life. The power of the mind, coupled with the support of a community, can lead to extraordinary achievements.

Clutch Performances: Players Who Excelled Under Pressure

Clutch performances are the epitome of excellence under pressure in baseball. These moments often define a player's career, showcasing their ability to deliver when it matters most. Picture a tight game, bases loaded, and the crowd on the edge of their seats. The pressure is immense, and only those who can maintain exceptional focus and resilience can thrive. It's in these high-stakes situations—whether it's a walk-off home run or striking out the side in a critical inning—that clutch performers shine. These players stay calm and focused and execute their skills flawlessly, turning a potential disaster into triumph.

One vivid example of clutch performance is Kirk Gibson's iconic home run in Game 1 of the 1988 World Series. Battling injuries that left him almost unable to walk, Gibson faced Dennis Eckersley, one of the best closers in the game. Despite the odds, Gibson stepped up to the plate and hit a walk-off home run that won the game and became one of the most memorable moments in baseball history. How did he do it? Gibson relied on his pre-performance routine, which included visualizing successful outcomes. Even though he was in immense pain, he mentally rehearsed hitting that home run, and when the moment came, his body followed his mind's script.

Madison Bumgarner delivered another unforgettable clutch performance in the 2014 World Series. Coming in as a reliever in Game 7, Bumgarner pitched five scoreless innings on just two days' rest, securing the Giants' championship. Bumgarner's ability to stay present and focused was critical. Between pitches, he used mindfulness techniques to stay grounded, taking deep breaths and focusing solely on the next pitch. His mental preparation was evident as he precisely executed each pitch, showcasing how staying present can lead to extraordinary performance under pressure.

The mental strategies behind these clutch performances are fascinating. Pre-performance routines play a crucial role. Whether it's a specific ritual before stepping up to bat or a series of deep breaths before a pitch, these routines help players settle their nerves and enter a state of focus. Visualization is another powerful tool.

Players create a mental blueprint that guides their actions by vividly imagining successful outcomes. This technique boosts confidence and prepares the mind and body to perform under pressure. Staying present is equally important. In high-stakes moments, the ability to focus on the here and now rather than getting lost in the magnitude of the situation can make all the difference.

The 2001 World Series provided another example of clutch performance. Derek Jeter, known for his composure, hit a game-winning home run in Game 4, earning the nickname "Mr. November." Jeter's mental preparation included a consistent pre-game routine and visualization exercises. He often spoke about staying calm and treating each at-bat the same, regardless of the game's pressure. His ability to maintain focus and execute under pressure made him one of the most clutch players in baseball history.

Players themselves often highlight the importance of mental preparation in their clutch performances. Mariano Rivera, the legendary closer for the Yankees, frequently mentioned his reliance on visualization and mindfulness. Before each pitch, Rivera would visualize the ball's trajectory and the desired outcome, helping him maintain focus and execute flawlessly. Even in the most pressure-packed situations, his calm demeanor was a testament to his mental fortitude.

In the 2016 World Series, the Cubs' Kris Bryant demonstrated a clutch performance by hitting a crucial home run in Game 5, keeping the Cubs' championship hopes alive. Bryant's approach to staying calm involved deep breathing and focusing on his pre-game routine. He mentioned in interviews how visualizing successful at-bats helped him remain confident and composed, even in the most intense moments. This mental preparation allowed him to rise to the occasion and deliver when his team needed him the most.

These stories illustrate how clutch performances are not just about physical skill but also about mental strength. Visualization, mindfulness, and pre-performance routines are essential tools that help players stay calm and focused and execute their best under pressure. By understanding and applying these strategies, you, too, can develop the mental toughness needed to excel in high-stakes situations, turning potential pressure into moments of triumph.

Success After Setbacks: Learning from Failure

Experiencing setbacks is an inevitable part of any athlete's career. Embracing failure as a learning opportunity is crucial for growth and resilience. When you approach setbacks with a growth mindset, you see them not as roadblocks but as stepping stones to improvement. This mindset fuels resilience, helping you bounce back stronger each time. It also builds character and mental strength, teaching you to persist in adversity.

Take the story of a high school player whose early career was marred by inconsistency at the plate. He often found himself in slumps that seemed impossible to break despite his talent. Instead of letting these struggles define him; he turned to reflective journaling and self-assessment. After each game, he would jot down what went wrong and what he could do better. This practice helped him identify patterns and areas for improvement. Seeking mentorship from his coach, he learned specific techniques to refine his swing and approach. Setting new, achievable goals, he focused on one aspect of his game at a time. Over the following season, Alex's performance steadily improved, and he became one of the most reliable hitters on his team.

In Major League Baseball, the story of Chris Davis offers a powerful example of rebounding from failure. Davis faced immense pressure and scrutiny after a record-breaking streak of hitless at-bats. Instead of succumbing to the weight of his slump, he utilized reflective journaling to analyze his approach at the plate. He sought guidance from hitting coaches and mentors who helped him adjust his mechanics and mental approach. By setting small, incremental goals, Davis regained his confidence and found his rhythm again. His journey from a historic slump to regaining his form showcases the importance of learning from failure and continuously striving for improvement.

Another compelling story is that of R.A. Dickey, whose early career struggles nearly ended his time in the majors. Dickey's persistence and willingness to adapt significantly influenced his comeback. After years of mediocre performance, he reinvented himself as a knuckleball pitcher, a rare and challenging path. Through extensive self-assessment and seeking guidance from seasoned knuckleballers, Dickey honed his craft. He set new goals focused on mastering this unique pitch and stuck to a rigorous training regimen. Dickey's transformation culminated in winning the Cy Young Award, proving that setbacks can be a launchpad for extraordinary success.

Reflective journaling and self-assessment are invaluable tools for athletes to learn from their failures. By regularly documenting your experiences, you gain insights into your strengths and weaknesses. This practice fosters self-awareness and helps you make informed adjustments. Seeking mentorship and guidance from coaches or experienced players provides additional perspectives and strategies for improvement. Setting new goals keeps you focused on progress rather than dwelling on past mistakes.

Consider the story of a college pitcher who faced a series of game-losing errors. Each loss weighed heavily on him, but he refused to be defeated. He started a journal where he analyzed each game's events, emotions, and reactions. He met regularly with his coach to discuss his findings and get feedback. With this newfound clarity, he set specific goals for each practice session, focusing on improving one aspect of her game at a time. His dedication paid off, and by the end of the season, he had not only improved his performance but also became a team leader, inspiring others with his resilience.

In baseball, comebacks are often celebrated as much as victories. Players who bounce back from failure demonstrate immense mental strength and resilience. Their stories inspire others to believe in their ability to overcome setbacks. Coaches and teammates frequently attest to the transformative power of these experiences. They highlight how players who learn from failure often emerge as more decisive, focused, and determined individuals.

Stories of Mental Resilience in Baseball

Mental resilience in baseball is the ability to bounce back from setbacks and maintain performance under pressure. It's that grit and determination to keep going, even when the odds seem insurmountable. One striking example of mental resilience is the story of a college player who returned to form after a long injury layoff. He was a star pitcher until a severe shoulder injury sidelined him for over a year. The road to recovery was grueling, filled with physical therapy and moments of doubt. But his mental resilience was unwavering. He practiced emotional regulation, managing his stress through mindfulness and breathing exercises. Positive self-talk became his mantra, telling himself, "I am healing; I will pitch again." Building a solid support network, including his family, teammates, and coaches, provided the encouragement he needed. When he finally returned to the mound, he was physically ready and mentally more potent than ever. His comeback season was stellar, earning him accolades and admiration from all who witnessed his journey.

The mental strategies these athletes use to build and maintain resilience are critical for anyone looking to strengthen their mental game. Emotional regulation and stress management are fundamental. Techniques like deep breathing, mindfulness, and journaling can help manage stress and maintain focus. Positive self-talk and affirmations are powerful tools to build confidence and keep negative thoughts at bay. Creating a strong support network is also essential. Surrounding yourself with people who believe in you and can offer encouragement and advice can significantly affect how you handle challenges.

In Major League Baseball, stories of mental resilience abound. One memorable moment is Jim Abbott's no-hitter for the Yankees in 1993. Born without a right hand, Abbott faced immense challenges from the start. Yet, his mental resilience was evident throughout his career. Abbott used emotional regulation techniques to stay calm under pressure, and his positive self-talk reinforced his belief in his abilities. His support network, including coaches and teammates, was crucial to his success. Abbott's no-hitter is a shining example of how mental resilience can lead to extraordinary achievements.

Another iconic example is the story of Mordecai "Three Finger" Brown, who overcame a severe farming accident that left him with mangled fingers. Despite this, Brown developed a unique grip and pitching style that made him one of the most successful pitchers in baseball history. His mental resilience was unparalleled. Brown's ability to adapt and thrive under pressure resulted from his unwavering belief in his capabilities. He maintained his performance through positive self-talk and the support of his team, ultimately earning a place in the Hall of Fame.

Players themselves often speak about the importance of mental resilience in their careers. Jon Lester, who battled and overcame cancer, frequently highlights how emotional regulation and a strong support network helped him return to peak performance. "I had to focus on what I could control," Lester once said. "Staying positive, taking it one day at a time, and leaning on my family and teammates made all the difference." Quotes like these underscore the significance of mental resilience in achieving and maintaining success in baseball.

These stories of mental resilience remind us that setbacks are not the end but opportunities to grow stronger. By practicing emotional regulation, engaging in positive self-talk, and building a robust support network, you can develop the resilience to bounce back from any challenge and maintain your performance under pressure. Whether you're facing an injury, personal challenges, or a tough season, these mental strategies can help you stay focused, positive, and ready for whatever comes your way.

Life Lessons from the Diamond

Baseball teaches us lessons that extend far beyond the diamond. The mental strategies learned in the game are invaluable in building character and developing essential life skills. One of the most profound impacts of baseball is its ability to shape personal and professional development. The discipline, focus, and perseverance required to excel in baseball translate seamlessly into other areas of life.

Another example is a high school athlete who used his baseball experiences to excel academically. He faced the rigorous demands of advanced placement classes while maintaining his performance on the field. The time management and organizational skills he developed through balancing practices, games, and schoolwork proved invaluable. He learned the importance of setting goals and creating a structured plan—his resilience and perseverance in overcoming slumps and setbacks in baseball carried over into his studies. When faced with challenging exams or demanding projects, he approached them with the same determination and focus that had served him well on the field.

The life lessons derived from baseball are numerous and impactful. Teamwork and collaboration are at the heart of the game. Every player must work together, each contributing unique skills to achieve a common goal. This lesson is easily applied to personal and professional relationships. Whether collaborating on a project at work or supporting family members through tough times, working well with others is crucial.

Resilience and perseverance in facing challenges are also critical lessons from baseball. The game is full of highs and lows, triumphs and failures. Learning to bounce back from a tough loss or a poor performance builds mental toughness. This resilience is essential in life, helping individuals navigate personal challenges and professional setbacks with a positive attitude and a willingness to keep pushing forward.

Leadership and communication skills are another invaluable lesson from baseball. Being a team leader requires more than just skill; it demands the ability to inspire and motivate others, communicate effectively, and make decisions under pressure. These skills are directly transferable to any leadership role, whether in the workplace, the community, or the home.

These examples highlight how the lessons learned on the baseball field can shape and enhance various aspects of life. The mental strategies and skills developed through the game—teamwork, resilience, leadership, and communication—are essential for personal growth and professional success. Baseball is not just a game; it's a school of life that prepares individuals for the challenges and opportunities that lie ahead.

As we move forward, remember baseball's broader impact and how its lessons can be applied beyond the sport. The game teaches us to be better teammates, leaders, and individuals on and off the field. In the next chapter, we'll explore how to build a holistic development plan for athletes, integrating these life lessons into a comprehensive personal and athletic growth approach.

10

HOLISTIC DEVELOPMENT OF THE ATHLETE

When I first started coaching, I had a player who was incredibly talented but often tired during games. He struggled to maintain energy levels, and his performance would dip in crucial moments. One day, I discovered that his diet consisted mainly of fast food and sugary snacks, and he wasn't getting enough sleep. We worked together to overhaul his nutrition and sleep habits, and the transformation was remarkable. He became more energetic, focused, and consistent on the field. This experience underscored how crucial proper nutrition and rest are for athletic performance.

The Importance of Nutrition and Rest

Nutrition plays a pivotal role in athletic performance. Think of your body as a high-performance car; it needs the right fuel to run efficiently. Proper nutrition provides the energy and nutrients necessary for optimal performance, muscle repair, and overall health. Carbohydrates, proteins, and fats are the macronutrients that fuel your body. Carbohydrates are your primary energy source, especially during high-intensity activities. Proteins are essential for muscle repair and recovery, while fats support overall health and sustain energy.

Hydration is equally important. Fluid loss of even 1-2% of your body weight can negatively affect performance. Staying hydrated helps regulate body temperature, maintain muscle function, and prevent cramps. The timing of your meals and snacks around training and games is also crucial. A well-balanced meal a few hours before a match provides sustained energy, while a small, easily digestible snack closer to game time can give you a quick energy boost.

For baseball players, specific nutritional guidelines can make a significant difference. Pre-game nutrition should focus on high-carbohydrate meals with moderate protein and low fat. Think of foods like pasta with lean meat, rice with chicken, or a hearty sandwich with whole-grain bread. During games, fluids and light snacks like fruits or energy bars are essential to maintain energy and hydration. Post-game nutrition should prioritize replenishing glycogen stores and repairing muscles. Foods rich in carbohydrates and proteins, such as rice bowls, pasta with ground beef, or a smoothie with low-fat chocolate milk, banana, and trail mix, are excellent choices.

Rest and recovery are just as vital as proper nutrition. Sleep is the body's natural way of repairing and rejuvenating. It is crucial in muscle recovery, mental clarity, and overall performance. During sleep, your body produces cytokines, which help fight off infections and reduce inflammation. Quality sleep enhances cognitive processing, memory retention, and decision-making—all critical aspects for any athlete.

The benefits of rest days and active recovery cannot be overstated. Rest days give your muscles time to recover and grow, reducing the risk of overuse injuries. Active recovery, such as light jogging or stretching, promotes blood flow to muscles, helping flush toxins and reduce soreness. Ignoring the need for rest can lead to overtraining, manifesting as persistent fatigue, decreased performance, and increased susceptibility to injuries.

Improving sleep quality is essential for optimal performance. Establishing a bedtime routine can signal your body that it's time to wind down. Activities like reading, taking a warm bath, or practicing relaxation exercises can help you transition to sleep mode. Creating a sleep-friendly environment is also crucial. Keep your room calm, dark, and quiet, and invest in a comfortable mattress and pillows. Limiting screen time before bed can significantly improve sleep quality. The blue light emitted by screens can interfere with your body's production of melatonin, a hormone that regulates sleep.

Sleep Hygiene Checklist:

- Establish a Bedtime Routine: Engage in relaxing activities like reading or warm baths before bed.
- Create a Sleep-Friendly Environment: Keep your room calm, dark, and quiet.
- Limit Screen Time: Avoid electronic devices at least an hour before bedtime.
- Consistent Sleep Schedule: Go to bed and wake up simultaneously every day, even on weekends.
- Avoid Stimulants: Limit caffeine and nicotine intake, especially in the evening.
- Stay Active: Engage in regular physical activity, but avoid vigorous exercise close to bedtime.
- Mindful Eating: Avoid large meals and excessive fluid intake right before bed.

Addressing these aspects of nutrition and rest can significantly enhance your athletic performance and overall well-being. Proper nutrition fuels your body, while adequate rest and recovery ensure that you are always at your best, both physically and mentally. These habits improve your game and contribute to a healthier, more balanced lifestyle.

Incorporating Mindfulness into Daily Routine

The results were almost immediate when I first introduced mindfulness to my players. I remember one particular season when we were struggling with inconsistency. Despite their physical skills, the players struggled to stay focused during games. I decided to integrate mindfulness exercises into our daily routine. To my surprise, the players showed remarkable concentration and overall performance improvements. At its core, mindfulness is being present in the moment. It involves paying attention to your thoughts, emotions, and surroundings without judgment. This practice can incredibly benefit athletes, reducing stress and anxiety, improving focus, and enhancing emotional regulation.

One of the key benefits of mindfulness for athletes is its ability to reduce stress and anxiety. High-pressure situations, such as a tight game or a crucial at-bat, can lead to overwhelming stress. Practicing mindfulness teaches you to stay calm and centered, even in the most intense moments. This mental clarity lets you make better decisions and execute your skills precisely. Another significant benefit is the improvement in focus and concentration. Mindfulness trains your mind to stay in the present moment, preventing distractions from affecting your performance. This heightened focus can differentiate between making a game-winning play and missing an opportunity. Additionally, mindfulness enhances emotional regulation. It helps you manage your emotions effectively, whether dealing with frustration after a mistake or maintaining composure during a heated game.

Integrating mindfulness into your daily routine doesn't have to be complicated. Start with morning mindfulness rituals. Practice meditation or deep breathing for a few minutes when you wake up. Find a quiet spot, sit comfortably, and focus on your breath. Inhale deeply through your nose, hold for a few seconds, and exhale slowly through your mouth. This simple exercise sets a positive tone for the day, helping you stay calm and focused. Another practical method is mindful eating. Pay attention to your food's taste, texture, and aroma during meals. Chew slowly and savor each bite. This practice enhances your enjoyment of food and trains your mind to be present. Throughout the day, incorporate mindfulness breaks. Take short pauses to practice deep breathing or observe your surroundings. These breaks can refresh your mind and improve concentration.

For athletes, specific mindfulness exercises can be efficient. One such exercise is body scan meditation. Lie down or sit comfortably and close your eyes. Starting from your toes, gradually bring your attention to each part of your body, noticing any tension or discomfort. This exercise helps you become more aware of your body and promotes relaxation. Mindful movement exercises like yoga or Tai Chi are also beneficial. These practices combine physical movement with conscious awareness, improving flexibility and mental focus. Guided imagery and visualization are powerful tools for athletes. Take a few minutes daily to visualize yourself performing successfully in a game. Imagine every detail, from the feel of the bat in your hands to the crowd's cheers. This mental rehearsal can boost your confidence and prepare you for actual performance.

Many professional athletes have successfully incorporated mindfulness into their routines. NBA star LeBron James practices mindfulness to enhance his focus and manage stress. He often uses guided meditation and visualization techniques to prepare for games. Tennis champion Novak Djokovic attributes much of his success to mindfulness. He practices yoga, meditation, and deep breathing exercises to stay calm and centered on the court. These athletes have found that mindfulness improves their performance and overall well-being. Testimonials from players who have adopted mindfulness practices further highlight its benefits.

One of my former players struggled with pre-game anxiety. After incorporating mindfulness exercises into his routine, including stretching, music and breathing, he reported feeling more relaxed and focused during games. His performance improved, and he became a more confident player.

Practical Mindfulness Exercises:

1. Body Scan Meditation: Lay down or sit comfortably, close your eyes, and bring your attention to each body part, starting from your toes. Notice any tension or discomfort and breathe into those areas to promote relaxation.
2. Mindful Movement: Engage in activities like yoga or Tai Chi. Focus on your movements and breathing, feeling each stretch and motion. This improves both physical and mental flexibility.
3. Guided Imagery and Visualization: Spend a few minutes each day visualizing yourself performing successfully in a game. Imagine every detail, from the bat's feel to the crowd's sound. This mental rehearsal boosts confidence and prepares you for actual performance.

Incorporating these mindfulness practices into your daily routine can significantly enhance your performance and well-being. Start with simple exercises and gradually integrate more techniques as you become comfortable. Remember, mindfulness is a skill that develops over time with consistent practice. As you cultivate mindfulness, you'll find yourself more focused, calm, and resilient on and off the field.

Long-Term Development Beyond Baseball

Athletes need to prepare for their futures beyond their playing careers because the reality is that not everyone will make it to the professional level. Even for those who do, athletic careers are often short-lived. Career planning and education are crucial. Start by identifying your strengths and interests outside of baseball. Maybe you have a knack for coaching, a passion for business, or an interest in healthcare. Knowing what excites you can help guide your career choices.

Developing transferable skills is another crucial aspect. Skills like teamwork, leadership, discipline, and time management are invaluable in any profession. You've honed these qualities in the field and can apply them in various other fields. For instance, the leadership skills you cultivate as a team captain can translate to a managerial role in a corporate setting.

Setting long-term personal and professional goals requires a strategic approach. Begin by conducting a self-assessment to identify your strengths, weaknesses, and interests. Once you understand clearly, create a career plan with specific milestones. For example, if you're interested in becoming a physical therapist, your plan might include earning a degree in kinesiology, gaining experience through internships, and obtaining necessary certifications.

Pursuing education and skills training is essential. Enroll in courses that align with your career goals, seek out internships, and take advantage of opportunities to learn and grow. Balancing sports with personal development can be challenging, but it's doable with effective time management strategies. Create a schedule that allocates time for academics, sports, and personal development. Use tools like planners or digital calendars to stay organized.

Seeking mentorship and career guidance can provide invaluable insights. Find mentors to offer advice and support as you navigate your career path. Former athletes, coaches, or professionals in your field of interest can provide perspectives based on their experiences.

Examples of successful transitions from sports to other careers are inspiring and instructive. Take the case of Curt Schilling, a former MLB pitcher who transitioned to a successful career as a video game developer. His story underscores the importance of planning and preparation. Schilling leveraged his passion for gaming and business acumen to build a new career after baseball.

Testimonials from athletes who have transitioned successfully to new careers often highlight the value of planning and preparation. They emphasize the importance of setting goals, seeking education and training, and leveraging transferable skills.

Balancing sports with personal development is not only possible but also beneficial. It ensures that you have a well-rounded skill set and are prepared for the future. Remember, your identity is not limited to being an athlete. Embrace your other interests and talents, and pursue them with the same passion and dedication you bring to your sport.

CONCLUSION

What a journey this has been! Reflecting on the years of coaching and the mental strategies we've discussed, I'm filled with gratitude and excitement for the path ahead. Let's take a moment to recap our book's main points and ensure you're equipped with the tools you need to elevate your game and your players.

In Chapter 1, "Foundations of Mental Toughness, " we laid the groundwork by exploring the importance of mental resilience, focus, and the power of visualization. Remember, a player's transformation through simple visualization techniques shows how mental toughness can improve a player's performance.

Chapter 2, "Focus and Concentration Techniques," delved into mindfulness on the field, in-game focus drills, and overcoming distractions. A player's story of staying present and executing a crucial double play highlighted the power of mindfulness in high-pressure situations.

Chapter 3, "Emotional Regulation Strategies," was about staying calm under pressure, utilizing effective breathing techniques, and harnessing the power of positive self-talk. A game-winning hit in the regional semifinals taught us the importance of emotional regulation in clutch moments.

Chapter 4 focused on "Confidence Building." We discussed setting realistic goals, using daily affirmations, learning from failure, and celebrating small wins. The transformation of our high school team through goal-setting and confidence-building exercises showed how these strategies can change a team's trajectory.

In Chapter 5, we explored "Parental Support and Involvement." We looked at creating a positive home environment, encouraging without pressuring, and fostering resilience. A story underscored the impact of positive parental reinforcement and support on a young athlete's confidence and performance.

Chapter 6, "Advanced Mental Strategies for High School Athletes," introduced advanced visualization techniques, handling scouting pressure, and developing leadership skills. We saw how our star pitcher used these techniques to overcome challenges and excel under pressure.

In Chapter 7, we moved to "College-Level Mental Strategies." We emphasized mental flexibility, peak performance techniques, stress management, and long-term goal setting. A team member's ability to adapt a mid-game approach showcased the power of mental flexibility.

Chapter 8 was all about "Effective Team Communication." We discussed building trust, resolving conflicts, conducting productive team meetings, and developing a team language. The player's vulnerability in sharing his challenges led to a deeper bond and a championship-winning season.

Chapter 9, "Inspirational Stories and Real-Life Examples," provided powerful stories of overcoming adversity, clutch performances, and success after setbacks. These stories highlighted the mental resilience and determination needed to excel in baseball and life.

Finally, Chapter 10 focused on the "Holistic Development of the Athlete." We discussed the importance of nutrition, rest, mindfulness, and planning for life beyond sports. A transformation through improved nutrition and rest underscored the significance of a holistic approach to athlete development.

The key takeaway from this book is that the mental game is just as important as the physical game. Visualization, mindfulness, emotional regulation, and confidence-building are not just buzz-words but game-changers. These strategies can help you and your players reach new heights on and off the field.

On a personal note, writing this book has been an enriching experience. It has allowed me to reflect on my 25 years of coaching and our incredible journey. The stories and strategies shared here are not just theoretical; they are drawn from real-life experiences and successes. They resonate with you and inspire you to cultivate a solid mental game in your players.

Now, it's time for you to take action. Start by implementing one or two strategies from each chapter. Encourage your players to visualize their success, practice mindfulness, and use positive self-talk. Foster a supportive environment where parents are involved positively. Build trust within your team and emphasize the importance of mental toughness. Remember, small steps lead to significant changes.

I want to leave you a final inspirational note to all the coaches and players reading this. *Baseball is more than just a game; it teaches life's greatest lessons.* The mental strategies you develop on the field will serve you in every aspect of your life. Embrace the journey, celebrate the small wins, and never stop striving for greatness. The power to succeed lies within you. Go out there and make a difference, not just as athletes, but as resilient, confident, and mentally strong individuals.

Thank you for taking this journey with me. I'm excited to see how you apply these strategies and witness the incredible transformations that lie ahead. Remember, *the game is won in the mind before it's won on the field.* Keep pushing, believing, and, most importantly, playing the game you love with all your heart.

REFERENCES

- Building Mental Toughness in Youth Baseball https://sportsedtv.com/blog/building-mental-toughness-in-youth-baseball
- 30 MLB Players Who Overcame Physical/Mental Obstacles ... https://bleacherreport.com/articles/1182893-30-mlb-players-who-overcame-physicalmental-obstacles-to-achieve-their-dreams
- Sports Visualization Techniques for Athletes https://www.successstartswithin.com/sports-psychology-articles/visualization-for-sports/visualization-techniques-for-athletes/
- The Role of Grit and Perseverance in Shaping Successful ... https://rooneybaseball.com/blog/the-role-of-grit-and-perseverance-in-shaping-successful-major-league-baseball-players#:~:text=Major%20league%20baseball%20is%20a,succeed%20at%20the%20highest%20level
- 20 Mindfulness Exercises for Athletes https://purposesoulathletics.com/20-mindfulness-exercises-for-athletes/
- High School Baseball Coaching Tips - How To Focus https://www.mentaltoughnesstrainer.com/high-school-baseball-coaching-tips/
- Teaching Young Athletes How To Refocus When Distracted https://www.youthsportspsychology.com/youth_sports_psychology_blog/teaching-young-athletes-how-to-refocus-when-distracted/
- Mental Training for Baseball https://www.successstartswithin.com/sports-psychology-articles/mental-coaching-for-baseball/mental-training-for-baseball/
- 9 Ways to Play Well Under Pressure in Baseball https://www.juniorbaseball.com/post/9-ways-to-play-well-under-pressure-in-baseball
- Sports Performance and Breathing Rate: What Is the ... https://www.ncbi.nlm.nih.gov/pmc/articles/PMC10224217/
- Optimize performance through positive self-talk https://www.hprc-online.org/mental-fitness/performance-psychology/optimize-performance-through-positive-self-talk
- 5 Winning Strategies for Managing Emotions in Sports https://purposesoulathletics.com/5-winning-strategies-for-managing-emotions-in-sports/

- The importance of goal setting for athletes https://metrifit.com/blog/the-importance-of-goal-setting-for-athletes/
- 50 Elite Athlete Affirmations https://purposesoulathletics.com/50-elite-athlete-affirmations/
- Fighting Back: 15 Athletes Who Have Battled Adversity https://bleacherreport.com/articles/429073-fighting-back-15-athletes-who-have-battled-adversity
- The Benefits of Coaching and Peer Mentoring in Youth … https://www.pheamerica.org/2020/the-benefits-of-coaching-and-peer-mentoring-in-youth-sports/
- The Role of Parental Involvement in Youth Sports Experience https://www.ncbi.nlm.nih.gov/pmc/articles/PMC8391271/
- Strategies for Building Positive Sport Experiences https://convention.shapeamerica.org/Common/Uploaded%20files/uploads/pdfs/2018/publications/strategies/Keep-Em-Playing.pdf
- Student-Athlete Mental Health: Tips for Parents and Coaches https://www.hopkinsmedicine.org/health/wellness-and-prevention/student-athlete-mental-health
- How to Effectively Manage Coach, Parent, and Player … https://thesportjournal.org/article/how-to-effectively-manage-coach-parent-and-player-relationships/
- How to Develop the Power of Visualization in Sports … https://thebehaviourinstitute.com/how-to-develop-the-power-of-visualization-in-sports-performance/#:~:text=Advanced%20Techniques%20for%20Visualization&text=In%20addition%20to%20visualizing%20specific,moves%2C%20and%20strategize%20your%20responses
- Dealing with Competitive Stress: Strategies for Handling … https://mpthreebaseball.com/blogs/news/dealing-with-competitive-stress-strategies-for-handling-pressure-in-games?srsltid=AfmBOooIPgXzbiSxNTZ4EZ1NCrHdx16JrYGqkxhwtV3qKdxB_au3B1MJ
- 5 Strategies for High School Athletes' Mental Preparation https://stellapop.com/unleashing-peak-performance-5-strategies-for-high-school-athletes-mental-preparation/
- Developing Leadership Skills on the Field: How Youth … https://mpthreebaseball.com/blogs/news/developing-leadership-skills-on-the-field-how-youth-baseball-can-teach-important-life-lessons?srsltid=AfmBOopgjrYkYBd1UHizysJQkk_SNar5WTMBadFc1CPggX0Eh1QagUIc

- Mental training for sports success https://www. mayoclinichealthsystem.org/hometown-health/speaking-of-health/ train-your-mind-for-race-day
- Training and Performance - NCAA.org https://www.ncaa.org/sports/ 2024/4/23/training-and-performance.aspx#:~:text=Promoting% 20adequate%20nutrition%2C%20hydration%20and,proper% 20hydration%20and%20restorative%20sleep
- Stress in Academic and Athletic Performance in Collegiate ... https:// www.ncbi.nlm.nih.gov/pmc/articles/PMC7739829/
- Long-term goal setting - Key planning information https://www.bbc.co. uk/bitesize/guides/zcqpbk7/revision/4
- The importance of trust between coaches and athletes https://coachad. com/articles/understanding-importance-trust/
- Managing Conflict on the Baseball Team: Resolving ... https:// mpthreebaseball.com/blogs/news/managing-conflict-on-the-baseball- team-resolving-differences-and-building-unity?srsltid= AfmBOooOJvL9m3dfq8HpOzIkMt2xEv6NmRFk Use9q2s63NNgMNIjtfpO
- Tips for Running a Successful Preseason Team Meeting https://discover. sportsengineplay.com/article/tips-running-successful-preseason- team-meeting
- The Importance of Communication in Sports | A-State Online https:// degree.astate.edu/online-programs/business/master-of-science- sports-administration/communication-in-sports/
- MLB Stars Past and Present Who Have Overcome the Longest Odds https://bleacherreport.com/articles/1317823-mlb-stars-past-and- present-who-have-overcome-the-longest-odds
- The most clutch plays in playoff history https://www.mlb.com/news/ most-clutch-plays-in-postseason-history-c212102298
- How to develop mental resilience in elite sports: https://www. innerdrive.co.uk/blog/mental-resilience-elite-sports/
- Ten life lessons learned from baseball https://probaseballinsider.com/ 10-life-lessons-learned-from-baseball/
- Sports Nutrition for the Student-Athlete: Baseball https://www. americandairy.com/dairy-diary/sports-nutrition-for-the-student- athlete-baseball/
- Sleep, Athletic Performance, and Recovery https://www. sleepfoundation.org/physical-activity/athletic-performance-and-sleep
- The Benefits of Mindfulness for Student-Athletes https://www. ncsasports.org/blog/benefits-of-mindfulness-for-athletes

- Athletes: Developing a Plan for a Meaningful Post-Sports ... https://moneysmartathlete.com/life-after-college-sports/athletes-developing-a-plan-for-a-meaningful-post-sports-career/